Career Choices
FOR VETERINARY TECHNICIANS

Opportunities for
Animal Lovers

Rebecca Rose, CVT, and Carin Smith, DVM

AAHA
press

American Animal Hospital Association Press
12575 West Bayaud Avenue
Lakewood, Colorado 80228
800/252-2242 or 303/986-2800
press.aahanet.org

Cover and Interior Design by Robin Baker

ISBN 978-1-58326-196-5

Library of Congress Cataloging-in-Publication Data
Rose, Rebecca, 1966-
  Career choices for veterinary technicians : opportunities for animal
lovers / Rebecca Rose, Carin Smith. -- Rev. 1st ed.
    p. ; cm.
  Includes bibliographical references and index.
  ISBN 978-1-58326-196-5
  I. Smith, Carin A. II. American Animal Hospital Association. III.
Title.
  [DNLM: 1. Animal Technicians. 2. Career Choice. 3. Vocational
Guidance. SF 774.5]
  SF756.28.R67 2013
  636.089'0737069--dc23

                          2009000298

19 18 17 16 15 14 13   1 2 3 4 5

Table of Contents

Foreword

A 2012 survey by *Parade Magazine* and Yahoo! Finance of 26,000 Americans found that almost 60 percent of those surveyed would choose a different career—that the majority of those Americans were unhappy not just with their job, but with their actual career field! I am always amazed at how many people I meet feel completely unfulfilled by their career, even those who are working in jobs that you would not think of as "dead-end" jobs. Most lack passion for what they do and feel like they do not have the opportunity to make a significant impact on their community in the place where they spend most of their waking hours—their job. My response to their grumbling? Find a career you are actually passionate about!

In a commencement speech for Stanford University in 2005, Steve Jobs, the well-known founder of Apple Computer, gave the following advice to the graduating class: "You've got to find what you love… Your work is going to fill a large part of your life, and the only way to be truly satisfied is to do what you believe is great work. And the only way to do great work is to love what you do. If you haven't found it yet, keep looking. Don't settle. As with all matters of the heart, you'll know when you find it."

Have you found "it"? Do you have a true passion for what you do? I hear constantly from students and graduate veterinary technicians that they have found it and they do love what they do! Whether it is saving the life of an animal that you weren't sure you could save, helping a veterinarian solve a tricky case, discovering the potential source of a patient's illness on a laboratory test, or assisting with a surgery that offers relief to an animal in pain, veterinary technicians consistently have the opportunity to perform "great work" in daily duties that are both challenging and interesting. While helping a devastated area restore veterinary services following a natural disaster, working at a specialty clinic that offers state-of-the-art approaches to treatment, participating in high-end research projects, educating the public about an endangered species, or contributing their training and talent in an underdeveloped country, veterinary technicians clearly know that they are making a positive difference in their community.

Not sure what all you can do as a veterinary technician? Then you have picked up the right book! In this second edition of *Career Choices for Veterinary Technicians*, Rebecca and Dr. Carin will share with you their insights and current information regarding the exciting opportunities available in the field of veterinary medicine — a field that, per the Bureau of Labor Statistics, reports "excellent job opportunities" and where employment is expected to grow "much faster than average" despite our country's continued state of economic struggle. I strongly encourage you to utilize their infectious enthusiasm for personal development and knowledge of the wide variety of paths available for veterinary technicians to research your options, whether you are trying to figure out how to turn a passion for animals into a medical career or you are a seasoned veterinary technician wanting to explore the range of specialization opportunities available. Never settle, find your niche, and you can transform your love for animals into a deeply fulfilling vocation!

Cynthia McNeil Medina, MA
Director of Student Services
Bel-Rea Institute of Animal Technology, Denver, Colorado

Preface

I have worked in the veterinary community since 1983, when I began working as a kennel assistant in a mixed-animal practice. Since that time, I have honed my technician skills, worked for both the state technician and veterinary associations, represented corporations as liaison to the veterinary team, taken on leadership roles within my state and national associations, encouraged technician and team utilization, given advice as a consultant, and loved my career choices every step of the way.

When I was a child of 10, I knew I wanted to be a veterinary technician. My mother worked for a veterinarian as his receptionist and assistant. I remember wanting to help with the animals after school. Thirty years later, I am still passionate about veterinary technology. You, too, can keep the passion alive for that long. If you are a parent, the years of child rearing can have their challenges, but those times are prevalent in nearly all careers. As veterinary hospitals grow and management becomes more attuned to the needs of all the women in the profession, there will be more choices about flexible work hours and child-care options.

While reading this book, you may decide veterinary technology is a viable career option whether you are a young student researching future options or a nontraditional student looking at a second or third career. If you are currently a credentialed veterinary technician working in a hospital and wanting to take your skills to the next level or seeking a career change within the veterinary community, one of the many choices outlined may resonate with you. You may continue to enjoy veterinary medicine and all it has to offer, fulfilling your needs—passionately, professionally, and financially.

Rebecca Rose, CVT, www.rebeccarosecvt.com

This book was created through collaboration unique to our times. I first met Rebecca Rose, CVT, through telephone calls and email. We discussed and then created a book together before we ever met in person. That first collaboration, on the *Relief Veterinary Technician's Manual,* led to a friendship and mutual respect as both our careers grew.

This new book, *Career Choices for Veterinary Technicians,* is based upon my earlier work, *Career Choices for Veterinarians: Beyond Private Practice.* Using that framework, Rebecca did the research to describe the career choices for veterinary technicians.

It is a distinct pleasure and honor to work with Rebecca, who brought tremendous energy and enthusiasm to this project. My wish for every reader is that you develop similar rewarding, positive, and mutually beneficial working relationships.

Carin Smith, DVM, www.smithvet.com

Introduction

Why a book about veterinary technician careers? Books about "animal careers" give brief descriptions of a large number of jobs for which there are few opportunities. This book fills a void in the literature—describing real opportunities for real jobs, for which anyone can become qualified with a two- or four-year degree. When it comes to "working with animals," veterinary technicians are uniquely qualified, not just for careers in private veterinary practices, but also for many animal-service jobs. As professionals who are trained to handle animals, administer medications, and work with people, veterinary technicians have unlimited opportunities.

How to Read This Book

Your approach to reading this book will depend on your current situation. Readers may already work in veterinary practice as noncredentialed assistants. Other readers may be students in high school or community college who are investigating career options. Still others are credentialed technicians working in private practice.

We highly recommend that anyone interested in working in a veterinary clinic pursue a credential (see Chapter 1).

Some readers may find that they have an interest in an allied position, such as grooming or pet-sitting. Such work could be done as a full-time career or as a sideline to your employment in a veterinary hospital.

Although a credential is not required for some positions described in this book, experience working in a veterinary hospital enhances your ability to be successful. For example, a pet-sitter who can administer routine daily medications will have more work than someone without that skill. Many people working on these allied career paths have also found that their work is more successful when they form networks or create a relationship with a veterinary hospital.

High school or community college students

Start with the overview of veterinary technology and the discussion of credentialing. Review other chapters based on your interests. Consider the value of attending an accredited veterinary technology program and becoming a credentialed technician to broaden your potential career options. The first four chapters are most important for you; then read other sections based on your interests.

Veterinary assistants

Are you facing a ceiling on your earnings or feeling that you want to do more in your current job? Review the information about private practice, credentialing, and specialty options. Take the "self-assessment questionnaire" in Chapter 2 to align your interests and your needs with your career path. The first four chapters are most important for you; then read other sections according to your interests.

Graduates of veterinary technology schools and credentialed technicians

You may be choosing your first job, investigating new options, or considering alternative paths for your career. Take the "self-assessment questionnaire" in Chapter 2 to align your interests and your needs with your career path. If you are currently employed but unhappy, you must explore your options. If you are dissatisfied with your job, do you want to stay in private practice but move on to a different hospital? Do you want increased responsibilities in your current job? Would you be interested in learning about different species or in pursuing a specialty? (Read Chapters 3, 4, and 8.) Or, do you want to consider options other than private practice? (Read Chapter 1, "Preparing to Enter the Job Market," plus other chapters based on your interests.)

No matter what, continually ask yourself if you're satisfied with your career path. As Kari Walker, CVT, says:

> I have not been a technician for long. I graduated …and started working as an overnight ER technician just a few days after. I was so excited for the Colorado Association for Certified Veterinary Technicians Conference, but I didn't realize that [a career choices] class would stick with me the most! …I wrote [as my goal] that I wanted to talk to my supervisor about my desire to learn more, do more, and be a more integral part of the team. By the time I received [the reminder] in the mail, I had earned the trust of my supervisor and was given my own drug box—pretty important in our ICU! I continued to let my supervisor know of my desire to be

better and to learn new skills. I have learned more advanced technical skills and recently I was able to place my first central line–triple lumen catheter in a feline jugular! …I feel like I have so much left to learn and that will come with time, but I have the sense of empowerment needed to express my desires to learn and excel.

Introduction to Veterinary Technology

Veterinary technology, as a profession, is a relatively new career. The first year that students graduated from veterinary technician programs was 1972. The profession today is among the 10 fastest-growing fields. A Department of Labor report projected growth at 41 percent through 2016 (see "Chapter Resources").

Jan Grace, LVT, MSM, was asked, "What has been the most rewarding aspect of your 29-year career in veterinary technology?" She replied:

> Watching the profession grow, pushing the growth. My class was the first class in Michigan to take the boards [exam taken upon graduation]. Then a few of us formed the North American Veterinary Technician Association (NAVTA); state associations were formed with another group; legislation was made within the Michigan practice act to include veterinary technicians, and a technician was appointed to the Michigan State Board of Examiners. NAVTA grew, the *NAVTA Journal* was created, and industry acceptance of technicians has grown. At times it feels like we are up against a brick wall, [while] other times of reflection show how far we have truly come as a profession.

The seasoned technician offers this advice: "The sky is the limit! There is so much opportunity out there. You have to have the willingness to find it, work for it, and take a few bumps along the way."

Veterinary technicians are integral members of the veterinary team, enhancing animal care alongside veterinarians, managers, receptionists, and technician assistants. Technicians perform an array of duties; they are trained to support the veterinarian in preventive health care, treatment, surgical assistance, anesthesia, and client education.

Sections of each chapter will give you details about pay, qualifications, and getting started in a variety of niches within veterinary technology. The following is a general overview of the profession.

Pay

Veterinary technicians earn salaries that compare to those in other fields requiring a similar education. Salaries vary according to experience, responsibility, geographic location, and employment type. As veterinary medicine explores new heights in diagnosis, treatment, and preventive health care, veterinary technicians will reach new heights as well.

Pay ranges for private practice are described in Chapter 3; other chapters show pay for different positions. Curious about current salaries, benefits, and skills required in a specific region? View www.salaryexpert.com. This Web site will focus your search by zip code. Both students and seasoned veterinary technicians will benefit from viewing this site. Referencing high and low salaries for a city will help identify expectations for that area, often providing a reality check.

You can also compare costs of living and salaries in different cities or states, since the same amount of money will buy you more in areas with a lower cost of living. Salary comparison calculator Web sites include www.cityrating.com/costofliving.asp and www.homefair.com.

Periodic salary surveys are conducted by professional veterinary organizations such as NAVTA, the Veterinary Hospital Managers Association (VHMA), and state groups. As a member of these organizations, you may tap into the results by viewing their respective Web sites and looking in the "Members Only" sections. In the September/October 2011 issue of the *NAVTA Journal*, you will find their most recent demographic survey. The American Animal Hospital Association publishes *Compensation and Benefits* for veterinarians, veterinary technicians, practice managers, and other veterinary staff. All these associations have compiled results that highlight trends, salaries, benefits, and much more.

Qualifications

Students graduating from an American Veterinary Medical Association (AVMA)–accredited program will learn entry-level skills performed in veterinary hospitals. A student graduating with a two-year degree earns an associate's degree in applied science (AAS). A student graduating after four years generally receives a bachelor's degree (BS).

For a complete list of AVMA-accredited programs, distant learning opportunities, and duties, view www.AVMA.org. As of 2012, there are over 190 AVMA-accredited veterinary technician programs, 21 offering four-year degrees and 9 with accredited distance-learning programs. Alaska, Arkansas, the District of

Columbia, Hawaii, Montana, and Rhode Island do not currently offer programs, although that is likely to change.

Evaluating a veterinary technician program

Students researching veterinary technician programs may want to answer these questions to assist in the decision-making process:

- Do I want an AAS or a bachelor's degree? Two or four years of college education?
- Where do I want to live? In which state or city? In-state or out-of-state tuition?
- What is the cost of classes per semester, per year, and overall?
- What scholarships or awards are given out? Is work study available?
- Do class credits transfer to other colleges? Is it a private or state-funded college?
- What is the reputation of the program?
- What percentage of students pass the Veterinary Technician National Exam?
- How many hands-on classes and labs are there?
- Do I want more experience with large animals? Does the program have horses and cattle on-site? Are there exotic animals on-site (reptiles, pocket pets, birds, fish)?
- How old is the facility?
- What opportunities are there for employment within the community while taking classes?
- Is distance learning a viable option?

About the Resources

Use the Internet and your local public library!

Resources are listed in each chapter, in reader-friendly format. Each topic/section has its own specific resources listed immediately after that material, if applicable, so you don't have to thumb through to a later section of the book to find it. In addition, you will find a resources list at the end of each chapter that includes items useful for all topics in that chapter. We have included comments about some of those resources to help you see what they offer.

Once you find a specific area of interest, you can go to these Web sites, associations, books, and articles for more details. (Web sites and locations of groups may change over time; enter the name of the group into your search engine to find current listings.)

You may also find books sold new or used through local bookstores or online companies. Some articles may be found online for free viewing, and others may require a payment. Use the Internet, but also use your local public library. Ask the librarian to obtain books or articles for you using the interlibrary loan service. This may be free or have a small fee, depending on your library.

Abbreviations and Acronyms

AAHA	American Animal Hospital Association
AAS	Associate's in Animal Science
AVMA	American Veterinary Medical Association
CVJ	Certified Veterinary Journalist
CVPM	Certified Veterinary Practice Manager
CVT	Certified Veterinary Technician
LVT	Licensed Veterinary Technician
NAVTA	National Association of Veterinary Technicians in America
RVT	Registered Veterinary Technician
VHMA	Veterinary Hospital Managers Association
VTS	Veterinary Technician Specialist

Chapter Resources

Bureau of Labor Statistics. www.bls.gov/oes/current/oes292056.htm. Provides information about average technician salaries.

Department of Labor. www.bls.gov/ooh/healthcare/veterinary-technologists-and-technicians.htm. Provides information on technician growth that projects 52 percent growth through 2020. Veterinary technologists and technicians held about 80,200 jobs in 2010. The majority worked in veterinary services. The remainder worked in boarding kennels; animal shelters; stables; grooming salons; zoos; state and private educational institutions; and local, state, and federal agencies.

National Association of Veterinary Technicians of America. www.navta.net. 1-703-740-8737.

NAVTA Model Practice Act for Veterinary Technicians. www.navta.net. 1-703-740-8737.

Programs in Veterinary Technology. www.avma.org/education/cvea. 1-847-925-8070.

State Laws and Regulations Regarding Veterinary Technician Credentials. www.aavsb.org. 1-877-698-8482.

Preparing to Enter the Job Market

The title "veterinary technician" has a specific meaning that applies to someone who has graduated from an American Veterinary Medical Association (AVMA)-accredited program or has become credentialed through appropriate testing. The typical technician works under the supervision of a veterinarian and performs a variety of animal health-care duties, such as preparing treatment rooms, restraining animals, administering injections, monitoring vital signs, preparing medications, performing lab tests, and assisting during surgery. In contrast, a "technician assistant" assists receptionists and technicians with a variety of tasks. Noncredentialed "technicians" are correctly referred to as "assistants." Only veterinarians can render a diagnosis, perform surgery, or prescribe medications. (Some exceptions exist in laboratory-animal medicine.) Knowing this distinction may aid in the decision to pursue a degree as a technician, a veterinarian, or both in a chronological fashion.

The roles and responsibilities of veterinary technicians are continually evolving, as is noted in a 2012 *Journal of the American Veterinary Medical Association* article: "AVMA President Douglas G. Aspros told *JAVMA News* that credentialed veterinary technicians are an integral part of veterinary practice today and that it's clear they can extend the reach of veterinarians in providing services to animals in a variety of situations. How they are used will develop over time" (Larkin 2012).

Veterinary Technician Exams and Credentials

New veterinary technician graduates from an AVMA-accredited school, with either an associate's or a bachelor's degree in hand, may need to take and pass national and sometimes state exams in order to receive their credentials.

National and state exams

Graduates of veterinary technician schools may take the Veterinary Technician National Exam (VTNE) upon graduation in order to receive credentials in most states. The American Association of Veterinary State Boards (AAVSB) offers the VTNE. Its Web site has a VTNE application menu explaining when the next tests are given. This score is transferable to states that require it. The Professional Exam Service distributes the test. The Technician Information Verifying Agency transfers test scores.

Some states require that veterinary technicians pass a state exam in addition to the national test. Each state sets its own requirements for credentialing, which may include an oral or a practical exam in addition to the traditional multiple-choice written test. You may find it beneficial to review the AAVSB Candidate Information Handbook found at www.aavsb.org/PDF/VTNE/CandidateInformationBooklet.pdf.

Review the AAVSB Web site, www.aavsb.org, to identify requirements for the state you live in or may move to. Search under the "Veterinary Technician" menu. Contact the veterinary technician program administrators if you have any questions (1-877-698-8482).

Once the state exam is taken and passed, you must pay a yearly fee to the state's governing body overseeing veterinary technicians (sometimes state boards, possibly a professional association) or simply register with the state.

Although it is a challenge, many technicians have taken and passed the test many years after graduation. You can do it, too.

There is a trend for states to offer reciprocity to technicians in "good standing." The governing body of these states issues a credential and sometimes may require a simple test on state rules and regulations.

Technician credentials

Credentialed technicians can be licensed (LVT), registered (RVT), or certified (CVT), depending on the state. Such credentialing is separate and different from simply passing the VTNE.

The current terminology recognized by decree of both the National Association of Veterinary Technicians in America (NAVTA) and the AVMA for a technician with any of those three titles is "Veterinary Technician." Multiple titles can be very confusing for the public. In order to simplify this, we use the term "Credentialed Veterinary Technician" to represent all of the titles. We use the word "credential" not only to denote licensure, registered, and certified, but also to imply an affective element inherent in these terms. NAVTA describes the technician credentials as follows:

Certification. The recognition by the private sector of voluntarily achieved standards. Certification is usually bestowed by a private sector, nonprofit professional association, or independent board of those members who achieve specified standards. Certification is therefore distinguished from licensure because it is generally nongovernmental and voluntary. Confusion can result when the title "certified" is used for a licensed profession, such as Certified Public Accountant. Many CVTs in the United States are recognized by government agencies such as boards of veterinary medical examiners, which also adds to the confusion.

Registration. Refers to the keeping of lists of practitioners by a government agency. It can be equivalent to licensure but may also be distinguished from licensure in that criteria for registration may not exist, and registration may not be required for practice.

Licensure/Licensing. Understood as the permission to do something as given by an authority, with the implication that one would not be permitted to do this activity without permission. To be licensed is more than a statement of qualification, as certification is. It is a statement of qualification, and it is the right to do a thing otherwise not permitted by a given authority. A government agency oversees licensure.

Both certification and licensure, however, carry the connotations of trust, belief, and confidence, for without these attributes the certification or the license would have little worth.

What about learning on the job?

Many people who have not attended a technician school still work in veterinary practice as veterinary assistants. The type of work done by assistants varies with each practice and also is governed by state regulations. In the past it was possible for such assistants to study "on the job" in order to take the Veterinary Technician National Examination (VTNE). However, now all candidates for the VTNE must be graduates of an accredited or approved educational program.

Pride in credentials

The growth in veterinary technology has fostered pride and professionalism that are enhanced by the credentialing process. Taking two to four years of intense training, and continuing to grow through education, specialization, and career advancement, are very important. Proudly identify yourself as a credentialed veterinary technician and educate the public, team members, and veterinarians about your accomplishments. Maintain your continuing education credits, seek to grow within your career, follow your passion, and know that many envy your career choice. Working with animals, veterinarians, medical teams, and the public is a very rewarding job.

The way you look, speak, act, and interact with others at work influences how you are perceived as a representative of one of the fastest-growing professions in the United States. The online Veterinary Support Personnel Network (VSPN) is a group offering specific continuing education for the veterinary team. One of the many classes it offers online is oriented toward professional development. Topics include specific aspects of ethics, understanding state practice acts, communication, team utilization, and career development. The *NAVTA Journal* and *Veterinary Technician Journal* also offer articles and tests that can apply toward your credits. (See "Chapter Resources.")

You may seek employment in government, industry, research, self-employment, management, consulting, publishing, or academia, to mention a few. You are limited only by your own imagination.

Secrets of Success: How to Apply for Any Job

Many veterinary technicians are successful and happy working in private practice; the vast majority of technicians are, in fact, in veterinary service. The details about other careers are meant for technicians seeking a new path. Students astute enough to examine their chosen profession—before they make a blind entrance—will benefit from reading about all the options available to them. Considering jobs in private practice as your only option could limit your opportunities. Instead, take a strong look at all your choices for greater long-term career success and satisfaction. Knowledge is power, and alternatives are the key to success. Know that there are many options available to you. The following tips will apply whether you are looking for a job inside or outside of private practice.

The key to success is persistence. Professionalism and integrity also enhance opportunities for success. Always view yourself as worthy of success; present a professional appearance, a positive attitude, and pride in your career and your achievements. Your skills and talents are valuable contributions to veterinary medicine. Persistently seek the career that fulfills both your financial and professional needs. When you are passionate about a job, it will evolve into a career.

Finding job openings

There are two methods of applying for any job: the "official written description of how to apply" and the "unofficial tips about how to get the job."

New graduates and seasoned Credentialed Veterinary Technicians (CVTs) have a good idea of how to find jobs. These openings are advertised in state technician newsletters and nationally distributed veterinary technician publications, as well as on Web sites specifically designed for veterinary teams and career sites. Many schools offer assistance in job placement to students graduating from a technician program. If it has been a while since you graduated, contact your alma mater to seek information on current job placement opportunities. Increase your job possibilities by posting your resumé on career Web sites (see below).

Job-Related Web Sites

advanstarvhc.com	careersniff.com	navta.org
animahealthjobs.com	craigslist.com	vetrelief.com
avma.org	indeed.com	vettechplus.com
cafevet.com	monster.com	vettechrelief.com
careers.com	myveterinarycareer.com	wheretechsconnect.com

Reviewing the *Veterinary Technician Journal* (see "Chapter Resources") reveals an amazing number of employers seeking credentialed veterinary technicians. The demand is there. How you promote yourself and design the career to meet your needs is up to you.

Experienced technicians know that many private-practice jobs are filled by word of mouth or networking. This is also the best way to find jobs outside of private practice. It is sometimes true that it is "who you know that counts." You don't have to be special to "know the right people." Anyone can do it. Here's how.

You will get the "official" word on how to apply for a given job in each section of this book. In addition to filling out the proper forms and sending in your resumé, there is another approach that works as well or even better. Before you go out and apply for a job, take a different approach. Go on an information-gathering expedition. The purpose of this is twofold: first, to actually gather information; second, to network—that is, to *meet lots of people*, and let them meet you. These contacts, over time, create a great resource for you.

How do you find these people? Begin networking at your state and local levels. Start with your city or state technician association. Also, view local Web sites, local newspaper advertisements, veterinary technician magazines (review the product forum and market news), and the national technician association's career center.

Call people who are doing the work that interests you and ask them if you can make an appointment to come in and talk about their job or their company. Invite interesting people to join you for lunch (you treat). In casual conversation, ask them about their duties and responsibilities and about what they like and dislike about their job. Don't ask for a job, but simply find out as much as you can. Be honest in telling them that you are investigating career paths and gathering information.

Association meetings

Another part of your information gathering and networking is participation in special-interest groups. Throughout this book you will see listings of these groups, which vary from state associations to national organizations that offer a variety of specialties and communication venues. Find out when these groups meet and attend their conferences. (Can't travel far? Find your city or regional association meeting.) Be ready to introduce yourself and start a conversation. Asking people about themselves is an icebreaker. You will then be able to meet a large number of people working in that field, and you will get an in-depth look at the variety of opportunities that may be available.

If you are considering options outside of private practice, plan to tackle the exhibit hall at a large veterinary meeting. Make your approach while lectures are in session, the exhibit hall is quiet, and exhibitors have the time and interest to talk to you. Prepare ahead of time by taking notes on the exhibits you're interested in—whether they be companies devoted to computer software, pet food, pharmaceuticals, or equipment. Generate a business card that you can leave with interested prospects.

Keep track of your contacts

No matter which approach or combination of approaches you take, be sure that you give your business card to everyone you meet. The card need only state your name, phone number, address, and email address. You needn't worry about having a job title on the card.

Once you have met a lot of people in different jobs, two things will happen: you'll have a much better idea of what's involved in specific jobs, and people will have met you and will remember you at a later date. Since you will be meeting a large number of people, make a habit of jotting short notes on their business cards to remind you where you met and what you talked about. Categorize them for easy retrieval.

Now you have the contacts and the information you need to send in your job application. You know a lot about the job you want, you know to whom to address your letter and application, and you know what the company needs. When your application crosses the right desk, that person will remember you. If there is a job opening, you might be the first person who comes to mind.

Social networking

Be sure to check various social media sites for information about job openings. While some businesses or associations have both Web sites and social media presence, others may have only a page on Facebook or another social media platform. Many associations and groups have a Twitter feed, and by following them, you can keep apprised of news and information. Also, create your profile on LinkedIn, which serves as a perpetual online resumé. While these are the current popular venues, remain aware of emerging new media that you can use to your advantage.

With all social media, whether you use them for personal interactions or business ones, you must assume that any potential future employer can and will see what you post. If you wonder whether something is appropriate, then err on the side of caution. While you are learning, less is always better. Until you get a feel for what is acceptable, watch more than you participate.

Your resumé, curriculum vitae, and cover letter

These titles may confuse some of you. Most people in the job world use a resumé to describe their job history and special talents. Professionals in academia are accustomed to using a *curriculum vitae* (CV) to describe their educational background.

The words *curriculum vitae* mean "class life" or "life study course," and thus the CV is a list of academic accomplishments. It is a document of the course of your studies and everything relevant to them—including all the classes taken, papers or books published, and grants sought and awarded. With the growing number of individuals pursuing veterinary technology as a second (sometimes even a third) career, there may be a few of you compiling a CV when applying for a new career job.

A resumé is an abstract of the CV plus any job history, skills, and experience that are relevant to the employer. It may include special abilities, honors and awards, and groups or associations to which you belong. The resumé is short: one concise page. Use of a resumé offers the advantage of adjusting it to suit each situation, while the CV remains as is, adding only further studies or grants.

Many people use a combined resumé and CV, where the resumé summarizes the attached CV and includes the information that is relevant to the employer's needs, whereas the CV shows only the academic information. The combined CV is better suited to the working professional in search of a position in a university or research program.

It is customary to include a cover letter with your resumé. Items that make your letter stand out include correct grammar and spelling, a description of outstanding talents, volunteer experiences, and interaction with the general public. Management styles differ; orient your materials to entice the manager hiring you.

Many books have been published about how to write a successful resumé and cover letter. Job Web sites such as wheretechsconnect.com, Monster.com, and Careers.com have pages offering assistance in creating a resumé. Studying them will help ensure that your resumé is the best it can be.

The interview

Dress for success! If you are thinking of wearing professional jeans and a top, upgrade to pressed suit pants and a jacket. First impressions truly can make or break you. Think of this as you prepare for your interview.

Here's where the pre-job-hunting, information-gathering expedition helps. One big worry is how to dress appropriately. If you've been in the potential employer's office before, you had a chance to see how staff dress, and you can match your style to theirs. Err on the dressed-up side. If you purchase new clothes for the interview, be sure to wear them prior to the appointment. Being "comfortable in your own skin" is imperative, and so is being comfortable in new clothes.

Role-play. Imagine you are in an actual interview for a real job opening. Hospital managers typically ask predictable questions. Make up a list and ask a fellow technician or supporter to role-play with you.

Interview the employer and hospital as much as they interview you. Find out whether you want to work for them. If you assume that you are qualified for the job (and you know this because you have done adequate research about the job opening, the hospital, or the company and its needs), then your approach can only be "of course they will want to hire me." Your goals will be (1) to show them why they need you and what you can do for them and (2) to find out whether you want to work for them. Be prepared to discuss your financial needs, too.

One problem that may arise is that you find a job for which you're ideally qualified, but it is not advertised as a job specifically for a veterinary technician. You may face the hurdle of changing your interviewer's stereotype of what a veterinary technician is before you will be seriously considered for the job. For example, a position may be open in a company needing an inventory specialist. Your past skills in a veterinary hospital will certainly transfer to the new company's needs. Veterinary technicians have found that it is necessary to enhance particular skills to succeed in specialized areas. Identify your passion and seek to fulfill that passion. This may be a necessary strategy for you to use to get a particular job; when it works, use your new position to reeducate your colleagues about the wide range of talents found in veterinary technicians.

Chapter Resources

See the Introduction for information on how to obtain these resources.

American Animal Hospital Association (AAHA). www.aahanet.org. 1-800-883-6301.

American Association of Veterinary State Boards (AAVSB). www.aavsb.org. 1-877-698-8482. Publishes a directory of licensure requirements.

American Veterinary Medical Association (AVMA). www.avma.org. 1-847-925-8070. Has many useful resources and links.

Ferrazzi, Keith, and Tahl Raz. 2005. *Never Eat Alone: And Other Secrets to Success One Relationship at a Time.* New York: Crown Business.

Fine, Debra. 2005. *The Fine Art of Small Talk: How to Start a Conversation, Keep It Going, Build Networking Skills—and Leave a Positive Impression!* Hyperion.

Honeychurch, Carole, and Angela Watrous. 2003. *Talk to Me: Conversation Tips for the Small-Talk Challenged.* New Harbinger.

Larkin, Malina. 2012. "Where to Draw the Line: Rural Practitioners Debate Role of Veterinary Technicians." *JAVMA News.* www.avma.org/News/JAVMANews/Pages/121001a.aspx. Accessed September 28, 2012.

McCurnin, Dennis M., and Joanna M. Bassert. 2006. *Clinical Textbook for Veterinary Technicians*, Sixth Edition. Philadelphia: Mosby.

National Association of Veterinary Technicians in America (NAVTA). www.navta.net. 1-703-740-8737. Offers a career center, the Model State Practice Act, surveys and nomenclature.

NAVTA Journal. www.navta.net/navta-journal/overview.

NetVet. www.netvet.wustl.edu/vet.htm. Contains a complete listing of links related to veterinary medicine, including careers, education, surveys, organizations, associations, publications, and more.

Office of Occupational Statistics and Employment Projections. *Occupational Outlook Handbook*, 2012–2013 Edition. U.S. Bureau of Labor Statistics. www.bls.gov/OCO. Accessed February 8, 2013.

Rose, Rebecca. 2011. "Overview of Veterinary Technology." *In Principles and Practice of Veterinary Technology*, Third Edition, edited by Margi Sirois. Philadelphia: Elsevier.

Veterinary Support Personnel Network. www.vspn.net. Offers a discussion forum and continuing education for veterinary technicians and other team members. View past chats under the "Library" tab.

Veterinary Technician Journal. www.vettechjournal.com.

Self-Assessment

Cynthia Medina, director of Student Services at Bel-Rea Institute of Animal Technology in Denver, Colorado, says of opportunities in this rapidly changing field:

> Consider the unusual options—I talk to many grads who are experiencing an exciting level of success beyond the basic hospital setting. If you want a change of setting, need more upward mobility, want a less physical job, or are seeking a challenge, consider something outside the norm to meet your specific wants and needs. These more unusual job opportunities are seen by the Department of Labor as an ongoing area of growth for the veterinary field. The "much faster than average" projected growth is going to continue to expand the array of choices and numbers of jobs available for trained technicians across the country.

Improve Your Resumé: Assess Your Skills and Knowledge

Whether you want to jump-start your career, broaden your responsibilities in your current job, make a move to a different hospital, or change your career path altogether, you will need to take stock of where you are. To improve your resumé and broaden your choices, think of yourself in a new way. Rather than being "just a technician," you have a compilation of skills and knowledge that is much broader than you think. Use your answers to the following questions to help beef up your resumé. Don't worry if only a few of these apply to you; the following sections will help you figure out how to acquire new skills and knowledge.

1. What were your jobs before you became a technician? Did you help out in a lab in college? Did you wait tables at the local diner? Did you manage a department in a discount store? The skills you learned while doing that work should be listed on your resumé. Many jobs in veterinary medicine require skills such as working with people, delegating, and managing.

2. What kind of volunteer work do you do? What groups are you involved with (not just veterinary groups but social groups, sports teams, Toastmasters, Rotary, parents' groups)? Have you ever been elected as an officer of any of those groups?

3. Have you ever written an article for a magazine, a pet column for your local paper, or a newsletter for your clinic or state association?

4. Have you ever spoken to your local schools or service clubs, like Kiwanis, or been interviewed by local television?

5. Have you taught 4-H classes or community classes for adults?

6. What specific things have you done as a veterinary technician? List your skills and areas of knowledge: radiology, anesthesia, surgery, pharmacology, toxicology, disease processes, medical terminology, and ability to read and understand complex scientific reports.

7. What about administrative and managerial skills? How many employees have you supervised? What duties have you held in managing a veterinary clinic? Be specific. Have you written a budget, handled employee payroll, hired and fired employees, created an employee handbook, or offered grief counseling?

Once you've broken down your experience into specific topics, you can see how diverse your knowledge and experiences are. Then you can start to see how your abilities can be applied to a wider variety of jobs than you'd ever dreamed. You may find that with some jobs the hiring agency may not be aware of the veterinary technician's training and thus the job announcement won't be one you'd obviously target. Let's imagine that the American Association of Equine Practitioners (AAEP) wants to hire an administrative assistant, offering a premium benefits package and advancement. This posting was not specific to a veterinary technician; however, some technicians do have the skills to fill the position.

This chapter is of particular value to seasoned veterinary technicians who are thinking of moving up in their career or changing their job. However, students should take note of this section, too—to get an idea of how veterinary technicians feel about changing their jobs. By anticipating that this could happen to you, you can avoid feeling that your life is ruined if your first job choice doesn't turn out exactly as you'd hoped, pay what you wanted, or fulfill your career goals.

Make a Positive Decision

For some veterinary technicians, thoughts of making a change start with dissatisfaction with their current jobs. However, to gain happiness in a new job or new career path, you must be driven by more than the desire to get away from your old one. It's time to turn dissatisfaction into desire. This book can help you find a new path that you look forward to entering. Enjoy your pursuit! Follow your passions!

What about going back to school? Do I need another degree?

One option when considering careers beyond general practice is to go back to school—to train in a different field or to specialize in a particular area of veterinary technology. This is the method of change most publicized, although it may not be the best for you. You need to make an educated decision. Begin now to research what is truly needed to make a career change. For example, becoming a Certified Veterinary Practice Manager may require a few added management courses.

Finances are a real consideration for everyone. Although returning to school means a longer delay before you can earn an increased income, the U.S. Bureau of Labor states, "technician students earning bachelor degrees garner higher salaries." What's more, you can defer some student loans until further training is completed.

The increase in income that results from further training is directly related to the type of work done. For example, advanced training yields far greater financial rewards for those who work in industry than for those who work in a university.

If you're like many veterinary technicians, you may not have the desire, time, or resources to go back to school. Perhaps you aren't sure enough of your potential new career choice that you are willing to commit to a couple more years of school. What's more, getting a new degree won't necessarily lead to greater happiness or success. Going back to school, in addition to all the expenses already incurred, sometimes is not financially possible, nor will it always have a good impact on your personal life.

School isn't the only route to a new career. You have many more options for change than you may realize. And you can get started in a new career without going back to school, to find out if you really like the change; then, later, you can always go back to school to further advance in your chosen new career (and sometimes your employer will pay for it!).

Although this book focuses on jobs that do not require more than an associate's degree, that doesn't mean that all veterinary technicians will qualify for all jobs, nor does it mean that further experience or training isn't required. However, you should move beyond the traditional "going back to school and getting another degree" mentality and see that your past degree(s) (AAS or BS), work experience, continuing education courses, internships, and independent study are acceptable ways to gain experience and become qualified for specific jobs. You can use your imagination and some creative time scheduling to achieve your own new learning situation. Don't immediately discount job ads that appear to ask for an advanced degree. We have encountered many people who said, "I didn't have the degree that's usually required for this job, but I got the job anyway because of my special knowledge/talents/experience." Close inspection of job announcements often reveals statements such as "BS or equivalent research experience" or "MBA or equivalent business experience." You might have just the specific experience and attitude they're looking for. Your positive attitude makes all the difference in the world.

Table 1: **Education Pays in Higher Earnings and Lower Unemployment Rates**

Unemployment Rate	Education Attained	Median Annual Earnings
	Doctoral or professional degree	$87,500
4.7%	Master's degree	$60,240
	Bachelor's degree	$63,430
7.0%	Associate's degree	$62,590
9.2%	Some college, no degree	$44,350
10.3%	High-school graduate	$34,180
14.9%	Less than a high-school diploma	$20,070

2010 data from http://www.bls.gov/emp/ep_table_education_summary.htm and http://www.bls.gov/cps/cpsa2010.pdf

Basic requirements for change

Whether you are moving up in your current job, pursuing a specialty, or considering a job outside of private practice, you will find your options improve when you acquire additional skills. Specific qualifications for each job are listed in the discussion of the job itself. No matter what the job is—whether in government, industry, or as a freelance technical writer—you must possess some basic skills and knowledge. These skill sets may be obtained in a number of ways, and not necessarily from a college degree. What you need, in almost every case, are the following:

- Computer skills
- Oral communication skills
- Understanding of business, including management skills
- Written communication skills
- Leadership and organizational ability
- A flexible attitude and a broad, diverse background

How are you going to acquire these skills? There are lots of ways to learn. Some cost money, yes—but think of this as "going back to school" in a whole new way. Consider how much less time and money this will consume than getting another degree!

Computer skills

All jobs require basic computer skills. Get your own computer and software. Play with it. Get comfortable with it. Many jobs rely heavily on computer use. For example, this book was researched almost solely through electronic mail, telephone, and Internet access. You can begin to gain these skills in any of the following ways:

- Take computer classes given by your local school, adult education night classes, or correspondence/online schools.
- Subscribe to a computer magazine.
- Read books and practice using specific software. Skills with Microsoft Word, Excel, and PowerPoint are highly recommended, as well as familiarity with common social networking platforms.

Understand the business

Learn about the business aspects of private practice to enhance your career. Do you know the business costs related to veterinary medical care, how fees are determined, and where your salary comes from? Do you know what it takes to be a team leader? Understanding basic business management will allow you to help yourself and the hospital for which you work. *Veterinary Economics* magazine is a good resource. (See "Chapter Resources.")

What about other jobs? When you understand the business end of your potential career field, you are better able to tell interviewers how your skills can enhance their company's goals. Studying can include reading (go to the library or search the Internet) and also talking to people. For example, if you want to write, you must understand the business of publishing. Before a magazine will pay you to write an article, they want to know whether it's useful for their readers and subscribers. If you want to start your own pet-sitting or -grooming business, you must understand record-keeping, taxes, insurance, and billing, among other things.

If you want to work in industry, you must understand business and sales. There are literally thousands of companies to choose from, in categories ranging from pharmaceuticals to pet foods to financial products. Attend veterinary and technician meetings, visit the exhibit hall, and chat with the representatives there about what they do and what their company's goals are. Ask them about their company's vision, mission, and values.

Oral communication skills

Offer to give presentations at your hospital's staff meetings, to local breeders' clubs, at veterinary and technician luncheons, or to your local service organizations. Keep a list of your speaking engagements for your resumé.

Join Toastmasters! We cannot recommend this highly enough. Toastmasters' mission is to provide a mutually supportive and positive learning environment in which every member has the opportunity to develop communication and leadership skills and to receive constructive evaluation, which in turn fosters self-confidence and personal growth. Toastmasters has programs for all kinds of people to learn what they need most in their jobs. Look in your local newspaper for meeting times. Clubs generally meet before or after work, once or twice a month. For the international Web site go to www.toastmasters.org. There is an opportunity to plug in your zip code to find meeting locations near you.

Written communication skills

Good writing skills are essential in any job. If necessary, take a course in basic writing (grammar, punctuation, business writing). Take a class in technical writing, magazine article writing, or other nonfiction writing given by your local school or online/correspondence courses.

Getting published can take your career to a higher level. Write articles for your state professional association, local breeders' club, or saddle club newsletter.

Write an article for a veterinary technician publication. Try *Veterinary Technician Journal* or *Firstline* (see "Chapter Resources") to start. As with other publications, these provide "author guidelines" that describe what they need and expect from a freelance writer.

A flexible attitude and a broad, diverse background

You can't buy these attributes, although most employers desire them. Will you be able to change as a job changes and as your employer's needs change? A diverse background is a plus in many jobs that require you to know a little bit about a variety of species and to be knowledgeable about technology, business, writing, and speaking. Employers know they can train you to do specific tasks if you are flexible and a lifelong learner.

Leadership and organizational ability

Get involved in your professional organizations. It is a very selfish thing to do, as you will get more out of it than you ever expected.

Volunteer to be an officer in your state veterinary technician association or civic group. The National Association of Veterinary Technicians in America (NAVTA) has a listing of state associations and state representatives. Help organize a veterinary technician meeting. Associations are eager for volunteers, and this is a very safe environment in which to grow.

There are many benefits from volunteering and helping. It has been found to boost self-esteem, increase energy, reduce symptoms of depression and stress, and create a sense of well-being. Studies find it may even increase your life span and contribute to better health (volunteers actually report fewer health problems than do nonvolunteers).

Volunteering allows you to try new skills and activities in a safe environment, increasing your options for future professions and leisure activities and contributing to your overall knowledge base. Volunteering makes you feel part of a team, accepted by peers who are traditionally caring, motivated, and supportive people. It allows you to develop connections professionally and personally, expanding your contacts, your LinkedIn connections, and your social calendar at the same time.

And finally, *you can quit*. This sounds like an odd benefit, but working because you want to, instead of feeling trapped by the need for a paycheck, allows you to thoroughly enjoy yourself.

Always remember the following: "Opportunities are the result of pluck, not luck. The people who succeed seek out opportunities, and if they can't find them, they create them" (Maxwell 2000).

How to get further education, skills, or knowledge

Use this list for general ideas. Specific educational opportunities may be listed in chapters that discuss specific career paths.

Externships, preceptors, and practicums

Hands-on training opportunities, such as externships, preceptors, and practicums, are not just for veterinary technician students! Ask whether you can spend a few weeks (or one day a week) working with someone for free or at low pay—in exchange, you get to learn on the job, meet people, and find out what is involved in a career you may want to pursue.

Institute a "technician swap" or "shadowing" between veterinary hospitals. It may be necessary to do this between different cities, in the event that some hospitals have confidentiality concerns. While attending a state gathering, ask if technicians are interested. Schedule a day of swapping, when you go to their clinic while they visit your clinic. This is a great opportunity to see what others are doing and to swap tips.

Home study/distance learning

This arena of learning is growing rapidly. There are courses on DVD, correspondence or online courses, and college courses via satellite television.

Visit the the Web site of the American Veterinary Medical Association (AVMA) for a list of the accredited distance-learning programs for veterinary technicians. There are currently nine to choose from, and the number will surely grow. The Veterinary Support Personnel Network (VSPN) provides ongoing short courses (see "Chapter Resources").

The American Animal Hospital Association (AAHA) also offers distance learning for technicians (see "Chapter Resources").

Workshops and seminars

AAHA offers continuing education at its annual meeting as well as intensive multiday courses at its headquarters in Denver, Colorado. Investigate the AAHA Veterinary Management School (VMS).

The Veterinary Hospital Managers Association (VHMA) has state and local chapters that offer education.

Attend meetings of the associations involved in your potential new career. Consider management meetings, extension agents' meetings, writers' seminars, and self-employment workshops. Use your imagination. How about companion-animal groups for the blind or disabled? These organizations work for a noble cause, helping the physically handicapped.

Adult education night classes

Contact your local community school or college. These classes are specifically geared toward working students. If you are self-employed, ask your accountant if the cost of your classes qualifies as a tax-deductible expense.

Military training

Enlist part-time or full-time in the military and apply to receive free training in a variety of fields.

Study on your own

Subscribe to magazines and journals and buy or borrow books about your area of interest. Read a book per week or per month as your time allows. CDs are great while traveling.

Intensive learning courses

Many colleges offer short-term (weekend or one to two months) intensive courses in a variety of areas.

Volunteer

Do volunteer work for a nonprofit agency. Seek out an area where you need experience: writing, speaking, or computer skills.

Explore your options and your limits

Are you thinking of leaving private practice? Before you zero in on a particular type of job, ask yourself some basic questions about your needs and your situation. The answers will narrow your potential choices for a new career.

Self-assessment questionnaire

1. **Am I (and is my family) able to move (to a different town in my state, to any other state, to another part of the world)?**
    Yes: Any career is open to you. If you enjoy travel, consider military or international assistance jobs. Or use your valuable life skills to teach at a veterinary technician program part-time or full-time.
    No: Eliminate most government and corporate jobs, as relocation is often necessary for advancement, or be ready to take a job that might not be your first choice, simply because its location is right for you. Consider relief work, writing, consulting (involves travel, but you can live where you want).

2. **Do I need a steady job with immediate good income and benefits (to support a family, get good health insurance, pay off debt)?**
   Yes: Eliminate relief (temp) work, starting your own business, writing, volunteer/assistance jobs, and consulting. Consider a corporate (industry) or government job. If you want to get further training paid for, consider the commissioned corps or another military position.
   No: Any career is open to you.

3. **Do I like working with people?**
   Yes: Most jobs are open to you. Focus on traditional private practice, teaching, consulting, industry technical service, and international assistance. Consider dog-training or -grooming options. Veterinary associations hire a number of veterinary technicians.
   No: Consider writing, computer jobs, or research and development in industry.

4. **Do I like working as part of a team or in a large group?**
   Yes: Consider private practice, management, corporate, or government job; working with organizations or associations; or a job with an international assistance group.
   No: Consider starting your own business, relief work, writing, and independent contractor work for corporations (sales, presentations, public relations liaison).

5. **Do I need action and movement, or is a desk job preferable or acceptable?**
   I need action: Consider traditional practice, dog training, specialty practices, lower-level state jobs (advancement means moving to a desk job; lower levels involve actual fieldwork); Animal and Plant Health Inspection Service (APHIS) jobs; Food Safety Inspection Service (FSIS) jobs; sales jobs; research and development for industry.
   Desk job: Look at corporate management, Environmental Protection Agency (EPA), federal or state nonfield positions, or writing.

6. **Do I want regular hours, or am I able and willing to work odd hours or days? Would regular hours feel like a "rut"?**
   Regular hours: Consider teaching, laboratory, research, government, or military jobs, or private practice in a city.
   Variety, odd hours: Consider relief work, starting your own business, writing, consulting, and some corporate jobs.

7. **Do I still want to work around or with animals?**

   Yes: Consider traditional practice, dog training, pet-sitting, relief work, animal welfare, industry, research and development, teaching, government, zoo, or a number of veterinary services. Think outside the box. How about starting an animal ambulance service, managing pets staying at assisted living facilities, or tending to K-9 patrol dogs when the officers are on vacation? Again, you are limited only by your own imagination.

   No: You can use your love of animals even if you don't work directly with them. Any job is open to you. Are you artistic? Consider creating cartoons for children's books related to the care of young animals. Are you organized? How about managing a veterinary technician association or working for any number of associations related to animals?

8. **Am I a new graduate, or do I have any private practice experience?**

   No experience: Choose a private practice where you will receive good training and mentoring. Consider government jobs, or if you are looking at industry, be ready to start in an area that may not be your primary interest, just to get your foot in the door. Do not consider management or relief work until you have a few years of experience.

   Experienced: Any job may be open to you. Explore your passions to determine what makes your heart sing and your wallet bulge.

9. **Do I want to live in a city or in a rural area?**

   City: Most jobs are open to you. Relief work is abundant in urban settings. Universities with laboratory settings are generally located in cities.

   Rural: Consulting or technical writing can be done from a rural home. Some industry jobs allow you to live in at least a small city, where you could find a home in the semirural suburbs. Extension agents often live in rural areas. Even the smallest of towns have animal welfare and pet adoption agencies. Some industry jobs allow you to work from home and, thus, live anywhere.

10. **Do I want to work for someone else? If not, do I have what it takes to run my own business?**

    Employee life is fine or preferred: Almost every career is open to you.

    Self-employed is what I want, being my own boss: Consider technical writing, editing, consulting, pet-sitting, pet training, grooming, or relief work. Many larger corporations will hire independent contractors for a number of projects. Getting your foot in the door is the key.

11. **How do I feel about paperwork, policies, and regulations?**
    Paperwork drives me nuts: Private practice, starting your own business, consulting, independent contractor, and relief work have some paperwork but less than industry or government jobs.
    I can live with paperwork: Private practice, specialty technician, management, associations, schools, the military, or government jobs might suit you.

12. **Make a list of the things you like and dislike about your current job.**
    Which of these will be different in your new chosen field? Which may be the same? Will a career change really bring you the changes you desire, or will it simply postpone your troubles, eventually leaving you with the same problems you have now? Feel the fear of stepping outside your comfort zone and do it anyway.

Re-evaluate your limits

For many people the primary restriction on life choices is geography. Because their family is living in one area or their spouse has a job that can't be given up, choices may be limited.

Others feel a need to continue to work with animals or to help people. Let's go through the list of "I have to's" and "I want to's." Look for specific information about these choices in the chapters that follow.

Personal-limits questionnaire

1. **I have to stay in my state. What are my best choices?**
   Private practice employment is an obvious option. Also consider relief work, writing, and pet-sitting. Use Web sites such as www.salaryexpert.com when considering relocation or completing school. After you enter your zip code, it provides the typical salaries of veterinary technicians and managers in that region. Contact the state technician and veterinary associations for listings of career options in your state. Visit state and national job Web sites listed in Chapter 1.

2. **I have to be close to my extended family. What are my best choices?**
   Contact your local Chamber of Commerce for brochures on businesses and activities in your immediate area. Attend the nonprofit association gathering

to see what organizations need volunteers. Animal welfare groups always need an extra hand. Begin networking with the local business and professional women's group. Get out there and mingle! It may be uncomfortable at first, but it will be most rewarding.

3. **I want to work with small animals.**
   Private practice jobs are available almost anywhere. What is it about working with animals that brings you the greatest joy? Animal welfare options are abundant. What aspect of animal welfare appeals to you: laboratory testing, surgical prep, comforting families when a beloved pet has passed away, or surgical recovery? Which resonates with you?

4. **I want to work with horses or horse owners.**
   Consider working for the state associations that support equine activities as an extension educator or agent, or for industry, with companies that supply equine products or services. Equine specialty practices are located in a variety of areas. Contact the American Association of Equine Veterinary Technicians for further information.

5. **I want to work with livestock, ranchers, or farmers.**
   Consider working for a volunteer/assistance group in international positions, state veterinarian's office, Agricultural Research Service (ARS), as an extension educator, or for industry, with companies that supply livestock products or services. Universities around the United States have research and development departments specifically working with ruminants such as buffalo, elk, cattle, and sheep. Ranch management is another option. Contact the American Association of Bovine Practitioners for further information.

6. **I want to work with or help people directly.**
   Consider working for a volunteer/assistance program, animal welfare organization, in grief counseling, or with emergency preparedness. Other choices are animal training, working with disabled children and horses (equine therapy), or with groups that pair dogs and children. Many service animals that live with disabled adults are trained for tasks such as turning on the lights, getting the phone, or pulling warm laundry out of the dryer. This may be the broadest opportunity yet, untapped for veterinary technicians. Surf the Internet for a variety of options.

7. **I want to work in another country.**

Consider relief work, volunteer/service work, military jobs, or federal jobs.

8. **I'm not sure I really want to change jobs.**

Ask for a leave of absence, and spend several weeks or months working with a volunteer or assistance group. The Peace Corps accepts veterinary technicians readily. Spend that time evaluating your life priorities. Or look into short-term educational opportunities, externships, or short-term fellowships that allow you to explore a new field without making a long-term commitment.

9. **I want to explore alternative modalities, assisting veterinarians practicing alternative medicine.**

A number of veterinarians throughout the United States work in positions that integrate alternative medicine. This is a rather new and exciting aspect of veterinary medicine. Review your state's veterinary directory to locate a hospital or veterinarian incorporating acupuncture, chiropractics, or massage into the practice. (See Chapter 3.)

10. **Geez, I'm stuck!**

- Are you placing so many limits on your job search that you have few choices left?
- Why can't you move to a different location? Can you move in order to begin your career change, with the potential of moving back to your desired area later on?
- Can you work as an employee until you gain enough experience to start your own business? Can you work two part-time jobs?
- Can you enjoy your pets and spend time with animals, even if a new career doesn't involve hands-on animal work? We suggest you get any job with regular hours and good pay, so you have time and energy to enjoy your own pets, train dogs, or ride your horse. If you'd prefer an active job but can't find one, will the regular, predictable hours of a well-paying desk job allow you the time and energy to exercise (and money for club fees, ski vacations, and sports equipment)?
- What are your priorities? What trade-offs are you willing to make?
- If you find that you've placed too many conditions on your requirements for a perfect job, then maybe there isn't one. Are you dissatisfied with your job, or are you dissatisfied with other aspects of your life? Are you searching

for an answer in a new job that cannot be found with a job change? Look within; know thyself.

Your search for the perfect job might result in the realization that the job you have now is the one that best fits your needs. That's great! Now you feel less like complaining, and you dwell less on your problems. Instead, you realize that your job is the one you'd choose out of all the choices in this book. You can now get on with it, making the best of your situation because you know you made a positive, conscious decision. Furthermore, you can read the next chapter about getting credentialed, if you haven't already. And if you'd like to make a little money on the side, you can read on for moonlighting opportunities.

Another possibility is that you truly want to make a drastic change in your career. Perhaps you want to study art, accounting, or music. Such a dramatic change takes a lot of thought. A safe way to explore a new option is to study it part-time while continuing to work in the veterinary world part-time, thus keeping all your options open until you're sure enough to make the change permanent.

If I'm not in veterinary practice, am I wasting my education?

Many of you will find success and happiness in private practice. But if not, one of the biggest stumbling blocks to avoid is the negative perception you may have about nonpractice jobs. Others may say to you (or you may say to yourself), "Gee, won't you feel like you wasted your time in veterinary technician school if you're not working in traditional practice?" I was even introduced once by someone in this way: "This is Rebecca Rose; she used to be a veterinary technician." I had to explain that I am still a veterinary technician, maintaining my credentials—I just make a living in a different way.

If you're unhappy, is it worth staying in a job just to prove that you didn't "waste" those years attending school? Consider this: You spent two to four years in veterinary technician school, with some of that time spent working with species you probably don't see in your current job, although it did give you a broad base in education. Is it worth staying in a job where you're unhappy, just to prove that you didn't "waste" those years? There are many options available to you, in private practice and beyond private practice.

Unfortunately, most people have a specific, romantic idea of what being a veterinary technician is all about. You may encounter disappointment from people who feel you aren't fulfilling your (their) dream. It's also hard to have a job that people can't immediately visualize in a positive way. When you say you're a veterinary technician, they visualize you working with a dog, a cat, or a horse. When you say you're the director of technical services for a pharmaceutical company, or that you do medical writing, or that you are a hospital manager, it's harder for others to imagine what you do.

Get ready for people to ask, "So, when are you going to go back to practice?" or "Don't you miss working with puppies?" Prepare your animated, happy reply to "What do you do?" in a few sentences that include a brief description of what you actually do for a living; for example, "I'm a veterinary technician, and like many technicians, I don't work in a hospital. Instead, my job involves [you fill in the blank] . . . I am passionate about my career!"

Another perspective on the "Aren't you wasting your schooling" thought: Aren't you wasting your time in a hospital if it's not what you enjoy? What do you prove by staying in a job just because it's what you thought you wanted to do sometime in the past? How will you feel two years from now if you make a change, or if you don't? Really look at your current state of affairs: Does it feel good? If not, what would make you feel better? What is stopping you from achieving your own happiness?

Chapter Resources

American Animal Hospital Association (AAHA). www.aahanet.org. 1-800-252-2242. Offers CE and more for veterinary technicians.

Bear, John, and Mariah Bear. 2005. *Bears' Guide to College Degrees by Mail: 100 Accredited Schools That Offer Bachelor's, Master's, Doctorates, and Law Degrees by Home Study*, Tenth Edition. New York: Ten Speed Press.

Bolles, Richard. 2012. *What Color Is Your Parachute? 2013: A Practical Job Manual for Job-Hunters and Career-Changers*. New York: Ten Speed Press.

Business and Professional Women. www.bpwusa.org. 1-202-293-1100. Promotes equality for all women in the workplace through advocacy, education, and information.

CityRating.com. www.cityrating.com/costofliving.asp. A salary comparison calculator; also see www.homefair.com and www.salaryexpert.com.

Colorado Association of Certified Veterinary Technicians (CACVT) Survey. www.CACVT.com/survey. Completed every three years.

Colvin, Jane. *2006 Earn College Credit for What You Know*. Dubuque, IA: Kendall/Hunt Publishing Company.

Criscito, Pat. 2002. *Guide to Distance Learning: The Practical Alternative to Standard Classroom Education*. Barron's Educational Series.

Felsted, Karen. 2008. "The Truth About the Technician Shortage." *Firstline*. Lenexa, KS: Advanstar Communications.

Firstline. www.firstlinemag.com.

Firstline. 2007. "10 Ways to Wow Your Boss." Lenexa, KS: Advanstar Communications. veterinaryteam.dvm360.com/firstline/data/articlestandard//firstline/092007/408676/article.pdf.

Firstline. 2006. "By the Numbers: 10 Signs It's Time to Find a New Job." Lenexa, KS: Advanstar Communications. veterinaryteam.dvm360.com/firstline/data/articlestandard//firstline/382006/373168/article.pdf.

Grabhorn, Lynn. 2010. *Excuse Me, Your Life Is Waiting*, Revised Edition. New York: Hampton Roads Publishing Co.

JAVMA News. 2007. "Workforce Study Examining the Breadth and Depth of the Profession." Schaumburg, IL: AVMA.

Johntz, Megan A. 2003. "Be Selfish—Volunteer." PsychToolBox.com. www.thestayathomeceo.com/whyvolunteer.htm. Accessed February 8, 2013.

Levit, Alexandra. 2004. *They Don't Teach Corporate in College: A Twenty-Something's Guide to the Business World*. Career Press.

Maxwell, John C. 2000. "Success One Day at a Time." Maxwell Motivation, Inc. www.hallmark.com.

National Association of Certified Veterinary Technicians (NACVT) Survey. www.NACVT.com/survey. Completed every three years.

National Council of Nonprofit Associations (NCNA). www.ncna.org. 1-202-962-0322. Offers helpful resources for nonprofits, including information on NCNA and the state associations.

Tilford, Monique, Joe Dominguez, and Vicki Robin. 2008. *Your Money or Your Life: 9 Steps to Transforming Your Relationship with Money and Achieving Financial Independence: Revised and Updated for the 21st Century*. New York: Penguin.

Toastmasters. www.toastmasters.org. A nonprofit organization that teaches anyone how to speak more confidently in any setting. View the site for presentations, courses, and location of groups nearest you.

Veterinary Economics. www.advanstar.com.

Veterinary Hospital Managers Association (VHMA). www.vhma.org. 1-877-599-2707.

Veterinary Support Personnel Network (VSPN). www.vspn.org. 1-530-756-4881. Offers networking and short courses.

Veterinary Technician Journal. www.vettechjournal.com.

Traditional Veterinary Practice

"I work in a one-doctor practice providing all the support I can. Anesthesia, dentals, diagnostics, IV catheters, handling and restraint, computer charges, hospital maintenance, inventory, reception help, and kennel help," said Scarlett LeBow, CVT, about her job in private practice in an interview with the authors. She has worked in a small-animal practice for two and a half years. The most rewarding care she gives is "intense nursing of geriatric patients." She recommends getting into a busy practice that extensively utilizes your skills. "I am finishing my bachelor's, but I can't imagine being anything else." She feels certified veterinary technicians need to be promoted to the general public and recognized as important health-care members, respected as human nurses are.

Technician Job Description

Careers in veterinary technology can be extensive and long-lived within the walls of veterinary hospitals. In fact, of the 80,200 technicians working in 2010, about 91 percent provided services in veterinary practice. The vast majority of technicians work in private practice.

Your review of career choices in veterinary technology begins with a discussion of traditional practice. This is what most people envision when they say "veterinary technician."

What does a veterinary technician do? The following descriptions are partially derived from the American Animal Hospital Association's (AAHA) definitions. We have also included definitions of other, related roles in the hospital.

The *Kennel Assistant* or *Animal Caretaker* feeds, exercises, and grooms animals while they are hospitalized or boarded; cleans cages and runs; and monitors animals for any unusual behavior or physical signs. The *Kennel Manager* performs many of the same duties as the kennel assistant, is responsible for the overall operation of the kennel, and manages kennel staff.

The *Veterinary (Technician) Assistant* assists receptionists with client service duties and assists veterinarians and technicians with examinations, performing treatments, radiographs, surgery, and lab tests. Noncredentialed technicians are correctly referred to as "assistants." There may be confusion among clients regarding the titles of employees in veterinary hospitals. Veterinary assistants, more appropriately called technician assistants or clinical aides, may have less education than the veterinary technician.

The National Association of Veterinary Technicians in America (NAVTA) recently began accrediting veterinary assistant programs. You may review their Web site as they add more programs to their list. Individuals graduating from an assistant program may sit for the exam and upon passing the exam will become an *Approved Veterinary Assistant*.

The *Veterinary Technician* holds a credential (see Chapter 1). The technician works under the supervision of a veterinarian and performs a variety of animal health-care duties, such as preparing treatment rooms, restraining animals, induction of anesthesia and monitoring, administering injections, monitoring vital signs, preparing medications, performing lab tests, and assisting during surgery. The *Head Technician* or *Technician Manager* performs these tasks and supervises the technician staff. The qualifications for veterinary technician positions listed in this chapter are the same as those described in the Introduction.

The term *nurse* is used at some veterinary hospitals to refer to technicians or assistants. There is some argument about the use of this term: Should it be reserved for those who serve human patients? Some states have laws regulating the use of *nurse*; know your state's position. (*Nurse* is routinely used in Europe and other parts of the world.)

The *Receptionist (Customer Service Representative* or *Client Relations Specialist)* greets clients; schedules appointments; enters client, patient, and financial data in the computer; generates invoices and explains them to clients; processes payments; and retrieves and stores medical records. The *Head Receptionist* or *Receptionist Manager* performs the same duties as the receptionist and manages the reception staff. (See Chapter 8, "Practice Management," for more.)

Small-Animal Private Practice

Traditional practice, in its narrowest sense, includes veterinary technicians who assist veterinarians operating a small service business that provides health care for domestic animals owned by private citizens. Health care includes preventive medicine, anesthesia, surgery, diagnosis and treatment of disease, nutritional advice, emergency and intensive care, and all other aspects of medicine and surgery.

The majority of veterinary technicians graduate from a two-year accredited American Veterinary Medical Association (AVMA) program. A small percentage graduate from a four-year program and receive a veterinary technology degree. Both programs educate the student to perform entry-level skills with exposure to a large variety of species of animals. Typically, students graduating from a four-year program receive further education in management.

Daily work

The small-animal practice (also called companion-animal practice) typically is confined to dogs and cats. However, many small-animal practitioners also work with birds, exotics, and pocket pets. Some hospitals concentrate only on exotics or birds, but this requires the large population base of a city. Large cities are the primary location of emergency clinics—veterinary hospitals open at night and on weekends. Trauma management and critical care are the focus of the emergency practice. Feline-only practices are becoming more popular.

A mixed practice provides services for a variety of domesticated animals: dogs, cats, horses, sheep, cattle, llamas, pigs, and goats. Many mixed-animal practices also work with exotic or pocket pets, including ferrets, guinea pigs, reptiles, and birds. The mixed-animal practice is the typical practice in small towns and across rural America. Since these hospitals are often the only ones available to the public in remote areas, the services they provide are varied.

Large-animal practice can be divided into equine and food-animal practice. Food animals include sheep, pigs, poultry, and cattle, as well as ostriches and other exotic species. Some clinics work with all large animals, while others limit their practice to one or two species, or even to a specific type of animal within the species. For instance, within an equine practice, services may be provided only to racehorses, show horses, or backyard "pleasure" horses; bovine businesses may work only with dairy or beef cattle (details later in this chapter).

Some states allow nonveterinarians to own veterinary medical hospitals. This may offer some advantages for the veterinary profession, such as higher employee retention, increased capital, and more selling options. However, many veterinarians are concerned that nondoctor owners may put more emphasis on money than on medicine. States can regulate facilities with nonveterinarian owners by using facility permits or registration. If you are a technician wanting to pursue practice owner-ship, contact your state government and local veterinarian professional association for information about regulations that may affect you.

Pay

The Bureau of Labor Statistics (www.bls.gov/ooh/healthcare/veterinary -technologists-and-technicians.htm) shows the average hourly wage of techni-cians working in practice as $14.28 in 2010. The American Animal Hospital Association's *Compensation and Benefits*, Seventh Edition (2011 data) shows these average hourly wages for full-time workers: credentialed technicians, $15.14; noncredentialed technicians, $13.18; and assistants, $11.18. As you explore your areas of interest, ask about pay while networking. Pay can vary substantially among various niches in private practice, and often no data are collected for each niche.

To start

Considering that there are approximately 30,000 veterinary hospitals in the United States, simply begin researching veterinary hospitals in your local area. The major-ity of veterinary hospitals now have a Web site and/or can be found on Yelp and even on Facebook. Veterinary hospital Web sites may have a "Career" tab. Your state veterinary technician or veterinary medical association may also be a resource. View their job postings. AAHA is a great resource, offering My Veterinary Career, powered by AAHA. Also, many of the professional veterinary organizations are linked with Veterinary Career Network.

Corporate Veterinary Practice

Veterinarian Andrew Murphie sold his seven-doctor practice to a large corporation. "It's kind of the best of both worlds," says Murphie. His retirement is ensured, but he is still practicing veterinary medicine and dealing with clients in the same manner that he has for 30 years. "They just monitor expenses a little more closely than I ever did" (*Virginia Business Magazine*, "The Rise of the Corporate Veterinarian, Growing Presence of National Chains in Virginia Reflects Dramatic Shifts in Industry," by Heather B. Hayes, August 2006, www.gatewayva.com/biz /virginiabusiness/magazine/yr2006/aug06/vet1.shtml).

Although any practice may be run as an incorporated business, the term *corpo-rate practice* has been used to describe a situation where several veterinary hospitals owned by one entity are run as a large business, often with branches in many cities.

The words *corporate veterinary practice, superstore, superclinic,* and *megapractice* have been used to describe these businesses.

There is no evidence that corporate practices will take over veterinary medicine. There will always be clients who prefer an independent hospital. Also, corporate entities generally limit their acquisitions to hospitals with a large number of clients.

Daily work

The basic approach of a corporate business is to reduce costs and streamline procedures so that veterinarians can concentrate on practicing medicine and surgery and spend less time running the business. Corporate practices may own many hospitals in many states. These corporations may hire a large number of veterinarians and veterinary technicians at a single hospital. That can save money when compared with the typical geographic area that has, perhaps, 10 different clinics, each with its own X-ray machine, surgical suite, and so on. Veterinary teams employed by corporate practices may receive superior benefits compared with what they'd get in the average private practice, which often doesn't provide any benefits at all.

Some argue that corporate practice reduces the potential for personal interaction between doctor and client or between doctor and staff members. Corporate practices tend to create policies in an effort to avoid inconsistencies among the teams' approaches. It is important to recognize that this occurs even in smaller hospitals, but there are fewer people involved in the decision-making process.

Corporate practices may offer a wider variety of products and services than do traditional veterinary hospitals. They may sell everything from dog toys to grooming aids. Some veterinarians view this approach as one that diminishes the professional aura of the team; others insist that catering to every need of the pet owner is simply good business. Corporate hospitals, because of their size, may utilize more management personnel so that the team can focus on medicine, surgery, and client service.

The bottom line is that veterinary technicians have choices. They can work in a high-tech, high-volume corporate facility or a smaller "mom-'n-pop" hospital. Both offer quality medicine. It is up to you to choose which fits your style and how you want to fit into the "veterinary family."

To start

Corporate veterinary practices tend to have strong recruiting programs. You may find booths set up at veterinary conferences. As an example, while attending a large or regional convention, you may speak with a representative from nearby VCA hospitals. You will see a short list of corporate hospitals and their Web sites. When viewing those sites, identify their "Career" tab to determine how to apply for their posted positions. You may fill out one application online and it may populate to many hospital managers throughout the United States.

Corporate Veterinary Hospitals

Banfield, the Pet Hospital	www.banfield.com
BrightHeart Veterinary Centers	www.brightheartvet.com
HealthyPet	www.healthypet.net
National Veterinary Associates	www.nvaonline.com
Veterinary Centers of America	www.vcapets.com

Large-Animal Veterinary Practice

Technicians who wish to work with horses, livestock, or other food animals will find a variety of job opportunities. A mixed-animal practice is one that serves all types of animals, from dogs to cattle. Practices may be limited to large animals (horses, cattle, and more), equine, dairy cattle, beef cattle, or small ruminants (sheep and goats).

Daily work

The work is often outdoors and involves physical exertion, although the latter is less of an issue than one might imagine. Good technique, understanding of animal behavior, and modern restraint methods make handling of large animals fairly easy. Rural veterinary practices that serve these clients will often provide emergency services; therefore, technicians might be asked to be on call for some weekends or evenings.

Food-animal medicine

Sandy Hass, RVT, has had a long and productive career. In 1987, she began working for Royal View Cattle at a feedlot west of Saskatoon, Saskatchewan, Canada. She worked her way up to herd-health coordinator. Her job was to oversee the health and nutrition of all the cattle on the lot. She was responsible for vaccinating, branding, and treating sick animals. She organized the cattle records, maintained inventory, ordered supplies, and managed a feed-supplement business. She highly encourages technicians to pursue a feedlot career. When working on a feedlot, you learn to recognize a sick animal before the disease progresses, so that the animal has a better chance of recovery. It's rewarding to see sick cattle get well and the mortality rates decrease. Sandy had the unique experience of quietly working with the animals while "cowboying up." Her entire story can be read in the *Veterinary Technician Journal* of September 2007.

Technicians work with food-animal veterinarians on small farms and at large production facilities. One article in *JAVMA* describes a model for use of veterinary technicians by food-animal practitioners. The authors suggest "using veterinary technicians to administer injections, collect feed samples, assess animal body condition, monitor health program indices, and perform other technical duties... Additional duties could include castration, dehorning, assistance with dystocia, repair of uterine or vaginal prolapse, venipuncture, hoof trimming, necropsy, collection of milk samples, and inputting and processing of data."

The authors propose that technicians could be used even more effectively; they could

> collect patient history and key objective patient data on the farm and then report to a veterinarian... The veterinarian would make a diagnosis predicated on these data (as well as any additional information requested) and then prescribe treatment. When the treatment is within the purview of a veterinary technician, the technician would provide that treatment to the animal. When the treatment is beyond the skill level or legal right of a veterinary technician, the veterinarian would proceed to the farm and provide that treatment. In this model, the use of veterinary technicians to travel to the farm, assess a problem, and provide treatment would allow veterinarians to pursue duties more appropriate for their professional trainin. (Remsburg et al. 2007)

Whether this model will become widespread (or whether it is currently legal under state regulations) is not certain, but it will probably be affected by economic trends in the United States.

Large-animal reproductive work

Technicians who enjoy working with cattle may perform artificial insemination (AI). Almost all AI is done by nonveterinarians and nonveterinary technicians. Either livestock producers or their employees do this work after they receive training from firms in the semen sales business. Veterinary technicians who are interested in this area should pursue employment by a livestock producer. One recent job announcement seen on Craigslist said, "Artificial Insemination Technician. Worldwide leader in bovine genetics is offering a position as an Artificial Inseminator in the Western Washington area. Compensation: $35,000–$45,000 DOE."

Equine medicine

Veterinary technicians interested in horses can work with an equine or mixed-animal practice. Work involves going to horse stables and horse owners' homes, restraining horses, and assisting the veterinarian with all procedures on the horse. Typical work includes reproductive exams, dentistry, treating injuries, and lameness evaluations. Some veterinarians focus on show horses, others on athletic competitors, and still others on breeders. Technicians working in an equine specialty practice may assist with colic surgeries, induce anesthesia, and monitor and recover the patient.

Anesthetizing and monitoring a horse under anesthesia are challenging. "I love the challenge that administering anesthesia provided. I was especially interested in managing pain during surgery, postoperatively, and in a successful recovery. Animals are so disoriented after surgery; I'd put myself in the horse's place by trying to understand its fear and bewilderment," states Deborah Reeder, RVT, in an article that appeared in the November 2007 *Veterinary Technician Journal*.

Deborah helped to organize the American Association of Equine Veterinary Technicians (AAEVT). She has been both an officer and the executive director. She devotes her time to working with industry partners, keeping projects on track, developing an online certification program, and editing the AAEVT *Equine Veterinary Nursing Manual*. She was instrumental in creating the format and structure for the specialization of equine nursing.

"Be the solution," advises Deborah. "Find an area that you are good in and specialize, promote your worth, and don't settle. I feel my career has exemplified that choice, not chance, determines your destiny."

DeeAnn Wilfong, BS, CVT, has recently been named the equine section editor for *Veterinary Technician Journal*. She was selected because of her exceptional contributions to equine medicine. She has worked in equine specialty practice for almost nine years. As section editor, she acquires articles for publication on current topics and trends in equine medicine. Veterinary technicians are able to receive continuing education courses through articles posted in publications, enabling technicians working with horses to stay current about treatments, applications, and rapid changes in the field.

Equine dentistry

The field of equine dentistry has grown and become more sophisticated. Work includes examining the horse's mouth and performing procedures such as floating teeth (filing off sharp edges). Work may be performed by veterinarians and/or veterinary technicians, depending on state regulations.

Controversy surrounds the practice of equine dentistry, and state regulations vary widely regarding who is allowed to perform these procedures. However, technicians in some states do perform equine dental procedures on their own. In an interview with the authors, Jim Wilson, DVM, JD, notes how different veterinarians and different states have varying rules regarding equine dentistry:

> It always amazes me how differently different state boards and the veterinary practitioners in such states handle this equine dentistry issue. In some states, the equine vets seem willing to give up this service and source of income because they don't have the time or physical stamina to do all that hard work. In others, they want to preserve this service so tightly that a veterinarian has to be within visual or audio range of any layperson doing equine dentistry. No wonder there is always so much confusion as to what the law, rules, regulations, and policies on this topic are across this vast country.

You'll want to be sure to clearly understand your state's rules and your local veterinarians' stances before you enter this field. You will have more work if you work with, not against, practicing veterinarians. Check with your state board regularly to ensure you know the current laws. As with small animals, a thorough equine dental exam may necessitate sedation, which requires a veterinarian's supervision.

Veterinary Technician Specialties

Jodi Kristel, CVT, VTS (Dentistry), was interviewed in *Veterinary Technician Journal* in April 2007. In this article, Jodi answers many questions about becoming specialized in veterinary dentistry, reveals hopes for the veterinary technician profession, and offers words of wisdom for fellow technicians:

> Until I specialized, I had no idea how little I really knew about dentistry! I had to start back at the basics and learn the anatomy of the mouth of each animal species. The program really raises your knowledge level and prepares you for everything that you're going

to see. I also believe that the VTS program makes the profession better in general and the clients are better served when they know that the person cleaning their pet's teeth has specialized knowledge. I am very pleased to see that more specialties are emerging.

Daily work

As you can imagine, when you are a specialist, a large portion of your time is spent in that specialty. As an example, a credentialed veterinary technician having a VTS in dentistry will spend 70 percent of the time on dental procedures. There is also an increased demand for continuing education with a dental focus, and there is a requirement for writing or presenting on the topic to maintain the specialty. Veterinary technicians who have taken their career to the specialty level have found it to be very rewarding—personally, professionally, and monetarily.

Qualifications/To start

Veterinary technicians in traditional practice may choose to specialize in one area of interest. For a number of years it has been projected that these technician specialists will be in high demand; this is a very exciting aspect of veterinary technology. Technician students may get a glimpse of specialties within veterinary medicine while they are in school; however, the requirements to become a specialist are best achieved after years of experience and written documentation of performed procedures. The National Association of Veterinary Technicians in America (NAVTA) oversees the veterinary technician specialties. Information regarding academies and societies may be found on NAVTA's Web site.

Veterinary Technician Specialty Groups

Academy of Equine Veterinary Nursing Technicians (AEVNT)
Academy of Internal Medicine for Veterinary Technicians (AIMVT)
Academy of Veterinary Behavior Technicians (AVBT)
Academy of Veterinary Clinical Pathology Technicians (AVCPT)
Academy of Veterinary Dental Technicians (AVDT)
Academy of Veterinary Emergency and Critical Care Technicians (AVECCT)
Academy of Veterinary Nutrition Technicians (AVNT)
Academy of Veterinary Surgical Technicians (AVST)
Academy of Veterinary Technician Anesthetists (AVTA)
Academy of Veterinary Technicians in Clinical Practice (AVTCP)
Academy of Veterinary Zoological Medicine Technicians (AVZMT)

The word *specialist* has a legal definition. A veterinary technician cannot be described as a specialist unless further training in the specialty has been obtained. Most specialties are organized within areas of medicine; however, the newly formed Equine Veterinary Technician Association may be changing that. Veterinary technicians who want to specialize go through rigorous training, meet very high expectations as outlined by the individual academies, and finally pass an intensive written and practical exam. Specialty groups are growing (see textbox on previous page). Visit www.navta.net for a current list.

Special Areas of Interest

Special areas of interest is the phrase used to describe those areas not included in NAVTA's specialty categories. A technician who does not hold a specialist credential must legally describe herself as someone with a "special area of interest," not as a specialist. Special areas of interest include a focus on a particular species or on certain types of therapy. Species-specific interests (wildlife, lab-animal medicine) are explored in the next chapter.

Know your state regulations. States vary in whether these approaches may be used by technicians on their own, by technicians only under a veterinarian's supervision, or only by a veterinarian. Rather than becoming irritated that you are not able to perform a technique unsupervised, develop a good relationship with an interested doctor or hospital.

Small-animal behavior

Technicians may pursue an interest in behavior in many ways. They may be involved with puppy classes in the hospitals where they work; they may become specialists (see "Veterinary Technician Specialties"); or they may pursue work as a trainer, either as a sideline or as a full-time career. Training as a career is discussed in detail in Chapter 5, "Starting Your Own Business."

Small-animal dentistry

Dental care of pets and horses is receiving increasing attention. According to guidelines published by the American Animal Hospital Association, appropriate dental evaluation and care of small animals usually require sedation or anesthesia and thus must be performed under the care of a veterinarian. Technicians interested in small-animal dentistry should seek out a veterinary hospital that performs these services.

Geriatric care/hospice/cancer care

Hospice and palliative care are becoming more important in veterinary medicine. Under the supervision of a veterinarian, technicians may become involved in home visits for pets in hospice care. Veterinary hospitals may offer this service, as may house-call veterinarians (see your local listings) or oncologists (cancer specialists in private practice or academia). Consider creating a pet hospice cooperative where neighboring veterinary clinics combine their efforts to provide safe chemotherapy and peaceful euthanasia. You may have seen or heard of pet owners not wanting to go back to the hospital where a dear companion was euthanized. A cooperative may relieve this burden.

If you are serious about improving hospice care services in your area, consider taking an intense weekend-long course to become certified in this area. Classes are being offered through the Two Hearts Pet Loss Center and other organizations. Further research may introduce you to many up-and-coming trends in pet hospice care. This may be one of the fastest-growing areas of veterinary medicine at this time.

Elizabeth Reed, RVT, CVT, CCRA, is working in a home-hospice/home-euthanasia business. Her title is manager/client service coordinator. She has this to say about her new career path: "Aside from the veterinarians working at Caring Pathways, I am the first hired employee. My job duties include building client relations with surrounding veterinary hospitals, scheduling appointments, providing in-home consultations, and doing basic management tasks. We are beginning to heavily market our company to other hospitals. I will be visiting clinics and sharing with them the philosophy and valuable services offered by Caring Pathways." She also says, "We are currently looking to open a hospice care center where clients can bring their pets for care and palliative treatment. The facility will be used for euthanasia procedures for clients that do not want the memory of their pet dying at home."

Many such businesses are owned by veterinarians, but it may be possible for technicians to run such a service. Rules and regulations vary from state to state, so do your homework before stepping out on your own. Where laws permit, technicians have created caring, passionate pet hospice businesses, offering extensive home care and performing euthanasia. Review your state's governing body's regulations specific to euthanasia and indirect supervision. Robyn Kesnow, RVT, began her business, Animal RN, to assist pet parents with at-home pet-care needs, which include home hospice care. She works closely with the attending veterinarian to help the family through the final stages of terminal illness and also speaks at veterinary conferences around the country.

Small-animal emergency and critical care

Veterinary technicians who enjoy a fast pace and working nights and weekends might like working in an emergency clinic. These clinics exist in most medium-size and large cities throughout the country. Emergency work has transitioned from just someone being available at night to its own specialty. While many of these hospitals employ "regular" credentialed technicians, some utilize the services of those who have received additional training.

Ancillary services

Many veterinary hospitals offer ancillary services that are not directly related to medicine. These include boarding, grooming, and training. Technicians may perform these services within a veterinary hospital or as a separate business. Working for someone else is a good stepping-stone to starting your own business. See Chapter 5, "Starting Your Own Business," for details.

Alternative/integrative medicine

Some veterinary technicians want to stay in private practice (traditional career) and assist veterinarians who practice alternative medicine. The term generally refers to areas such as veterinary chiropractic, homeopathy, massage, and acupuncture. The scope of alternative medicine changes over time, as formerly alternative practices blend into mainstream medicine. A new term, "integrative medicine," more closely reflects the current approach to blending new and old approaches.

Nutrition is one of the most popular alternative modalities. Pet food companies vie for your attention by offering courses in nutrition, both online and through veterinary practices. These courses are often quite good but, of course, always combine corporate-sponsored learning with independent information.

Identify veterinarians specializing in alternative or integrative medicine and speak with them about how you may support their practice. Several groups offer information and courses for veterinary technicians who are interested.

Many terms relating to these approaches are misunderstood and misused. Learn the correct definitions of all these terms so you are clear about each. For example, many doctors use solely "Western" medicine and yet take a "holistic" approach, which means they consider all factors that may influence the animal's health.

Rehabilitation therapy

Some prefer that the popular term *physical therapy* be reserved for people, and that *rehabilitation therapy* be used to describe the application of these techniques to animals. According to *AAHA Pain Management Guidelines for Dogs and Cats*, "rehabilitation" includes techniques such as cryotherapy, heat therapy, massage, stretching, passive range-of-motion exercise, hydrotherapy, therapeutic exercise, use of dryland or underwater treadmill, and strength building. A few veterinary hospitals in large cities have installed therapeutic swimming pools and other equipment to focus on rehabilitation.

The University of Tennessee's Outreach and Continuing Education department offers a certificate program in canine physical rehabilitation. This program is a sequence of postgraduate courses (offered in various locations) for veterinarians, physical therapists, physical therapist assistants, and veterinary technicians or students of these professions, followed by a supervised clinical experience and a cumulative examination.

Definitions *(Mosby's Medical Dictionary)*

Holistic: Pertaining to the whole; considering all factors.

Holistic health care (human medicine): A system of comprehensive or total patient care that considers the physical, emotional, social, economic, and spiritual needs of the person; his or her response to illness; and the effect of the illness on the ability to meet self-care needs.

Homeopathy: A system of therapeutics based on the theory that "like cures like"; the thought is that a large amount of a particular drug may cause symptoms of a disease, a moderate dose may reduce those symptoms, and thus disease symptoms could be cured by very small doses of that medicine. Little if any evidence exists to support the effectiveness of homeopathy.

Massage: The manipulation of the soft tissue of the body through stroking, rubbing, kneading, or tapping to increase circulation, improve muscle tone, and relax the patient. Some state regulators differentiate between "massage" and "massage therapy." The latter may be considered to be the practice of medicine, and thus must be done by or under the supervision of a veterinarian, depending on state law.

Physical therapy: The treatment of disorders with physical agents and methods, such as massage, manipulation, exercises, cold, heat (including ultrasonic heat), hydrotherapy, electrical stimulation, and light, to assist in rehabilitating patients after an illness or injury.

Rehabilitation therapy: The application of physical therapy techniques to animals.

Animal massage

Animal massage is a hot topic, and there is some controversy around credentialing. When performed by someone who is not a veterinarian, it is recommended that the word *therapy* not be used, since *massage therapy* implies medical expertise. The preferred term is *animal massage.*

State laws vary, from those not mentioning massage at all to those that specifically limit its use. Review your own state regulations to be sure you understand your responsibilities and limits. All states are separately governed, and animal massage is one arena that will go through regulation changes in this decade. There is currently no national standard for certification in animal massage, although it is likely that this will occur.

People performing animal massage may work with veterinarians or on their own. Veterinarians become concerned when massage is performed without a veterinarian's involvement. They are concerned that an accurate diagnosis be made prior to using any treatment or management approach. It is possible that an injury could persist or worsen if an animal receives inappropriate treatment. In order to meet the highest standards in the field, you should look into a reputable animal massage program. As written in *Equissage*, "Massaging a dog, horse, or cat is not the same as massaging a human. To require an animal massage therapist to first learn how to massage humans would be akin to requiring a veterinarian to first attend medical school before practicing on animals."

A large number of canine and equine massage "therapy" programs throughout the United States offer certification. Be sure to review credentialing and reputable sources for course quality.

Chapter Resources

Many veterinary associations have member directories in which you may find veterinary practices and potential jobs. Many associations also hold meetings with continuing education on various topics. Also included in this list are books, articles, and Web sites.

American Association of Feline Practitioners (AAFP). www.aafponline.org. 1-800-874-0498.

American Veterinary Medical Association (AVMA). www.avma.org. 1-847-925-8070. Offers an exhaustive list of veterinary special-interest groups. Your state veterinary directory may list veterinarians by specialty. The AVMA also has current information about "scope of practice," which refers to procedures that must be done by a licensed veterinarian. Also view the AVMA brochure "Careers in Veterinary Technology" and AVMA position statements.

AVMA. 2008. "Scope-of-Practice Laws Draw Attacks: Laypersons Challenge Veterinary State Boards in Court." *JAVMA News*, October.

Directory of Veterinary State Practice Acts. American Association of Veterinary State Boards. www.aavsb.org/DLR/DLR.asp. 1-877-698-8482.

Equissage, www.equissage.com. 1-800-843-0024.

Wilson, Jim, and Perri Stark. 2000. "Should Non-doctors Own Practices?" *Veterinary Economics*. Lenexa, KS: Advanstar Communications.

Small–Animal Private Practice

AAHA. *Compensation & Benefits*. Lakewood, CO: AAHA Press. Published biannually.

American Animal Hospital Association (AAHA). www.aahanet.org. 1-800-883-6301. Offers accreditation to companion-animal hospitals that meet certain criteria.

American Association of Feline Practitioners (AAFP). www.aafponline.org. 1-800-874-0498. Represents veterinary hospitals and veterinarians who focus on cats.

Corporate Veterinary Hospitals

Glassman, Gary. 2007. "The New Era of Corporate Practice." *Veterinary Economics*, November. www.veterinarybusiness.dvm360.com/vetec/article/articleDetail. Interesting facts regarding purchasing and statistics.

Hayes, Heather B. 2006. "The Rise of the Corporate Veterinarian: Growing Presence of National Chains in Virginia Reflects Shifts in Industry." *Virginia Business News*, August. www.virginiabusiness.com/edit/magazine/yr2006/aug06/vet2.shtml.

Food Animals

American Association of Bovine Practitioners (AABP). www.aabp.org. 1-334-821-0042.

Remsburg, Darren W., et al. 2007. "A Proposed Novel Food Animal Health Care Delivery System." *JAVMA*, September 15.

Veterinary Technician Journal. 2007. "Making a Difference: A Talk with Sandy Hass, RVT." *Veterinary Technician Journal*, September.

Equine Medicine

Academy of Equine Veterinary Nursing Technicians (AEVNT). www.aaevt.org/aaevtacademy.html.

American Association of Equine Practitioners (AAEP). www.aaep.org. 1-859-233-0147. Offers courses specifically for technicians and an annual meeting for education and networking.

Donavon, Liz. 2008. "Giving Back: A Talk with Debbie Reed, BS, RVT." *Veterinary Technician Journal*, June.

Vardaro Tucker, Andrea. 2007. "Leaping to Great Heighths: A Talk with Deborah Reeder, RVT." *Veterinary Technician Journal*, November.

Equine Dentistry

American Association of Equine Veterinary Technicians. www.aaevt.org. 1-214-505-1548. A group of technicians focusing on equine technician specialties.

International Association of Equine Dentistry. www.iaedonline.com. Offers various levels of certification in equine dentistry. Technicians may be members.

Specialties

National Association of Veterinary Technicians in America (NAVTA). www.navta.net. Lists academies and societies offering specialty requirements and exams for technicians.

Behavior

Academy of Veterinary Behavior Technicians. www.svbt.org.

American Veterinary Society of Animal Behavior. www.avsabonline.org.

Small–Animal Dentistry

AAHA Dental Care Guidelines for Dogs and Cats. www.aahanet.org/resources /guidelines.aspx. 1-800-883-6301.

Academy of Veterinary Dental Technicians. www.avdt.us.

American Veterinary Dental College. www.avdc.org. 1-856-229-7696.

Donovan, L. 2007. "Charting a Path to Success: A Talk with Jodi Kristel, CVT, VTS (Dentistry)." *Veterinary Technician Journal*, April.

Geriatric, Hospice, and Cancer Care

Anderson, Cheryl. 2010. "Terminally Ill Pets and Their Grieving Families Find Comfort in Hands of Hospice." *Good Grief Pet Loss* Blog, May 2. www.goodgriefpetloss. wordpress.com/2010/05/03/pet-hospice-offers-quality-at-the-end-of-a-pets-life. Accessed February 8, 2013.

Animal Hospice. www.animalhospice.org. 1-208-726-9606. Offers information for pet owners about hospice care; also see www.spiritsintransition.org, 1-805-598-6496.

Annual Symposium on Veterinary Hospice Care. www.pethospice.org. 1-707-557-8595.

AVMA. "AVMA Guidelines for Veterinary Hospice Care." American Veterinary Medical Association. www.avma.org/KB/Policies/Pages/Guidelines-for-Veterinary-Hospice -Care.aspx.

Colorado State University's Animal Cancer Center. www.animalcancercenter.org. 1-970-297-4195. Has many ongoing trial cases to enhance the veterinary community's understanding of cancer, pets, and the human-animal bond.

Delta Society. www.deltasociety.org. 1-425-679-5500. The leading international resource for information about the human-animal bond, validating the important roles animals play in our lives.

International Association for Animal Hospice and Palliative Care. www.iaahpc.org.

JAVMA. 2006. "More Veterinarians Offer Hospice Care for Pets." *JAVMA News,* August.

Two Hearts Pet Loss Center. www.pet-loss-grief.com. Offers a pet loss and grief companioning certification.

Veterinary Cancer Society and Veterinary Technician Cancer Society. www.vetceteraancersociety.org. 1-619-474-8929. Has a Web page for technicians interested in this field.

Emergency Care

Academy of Veterinary Emergency Critical Care Technicians. www.avecct.org.

AVECCT. "Credential Requirements." www.avecct.org/content/credential_requirements.

Veterinary Emergency and Critical Care Society. www.veccs.org. 1-210-698-5575.

Alternative Therapy

Academy of Veterinary Homeopathy. www.theavh.org.

American Holistic Veterinary Medical Association. www.ahvma.org. 1-410-569-0795.

American Veterinary Chiropractic Association. www.animalchiropractic.org. 1-918-784-2231.

Bernard, Shari. 1995. "Animal-Assisted Therapy: A Guide for Health Care Professionals and Volunteers." *Therapet.*

Hamilton, Don. 1999. *Homeopathic Care for Cats and Dogs: Small Doses for Small Animals.* North Atlantic Books.

International Veterinary Acupuncture Society. www.ivas.org. 1-970-966-0666.

National Board of Certification for Animal Acupressure & Massage (NBCAAM). www.nbcaam.net. info@nbcaam.net. Provides a "Scope of Practice" and "Code of Ethics" for animal massage and acupressure, committee listings, and other resources.

Schoen, Allen M. 2001. *Veterinary Acupuncture: Ancient Art to Modern Medicine.* Philadelphia: Mosby.

Shojai, Amy. 2001. *New Choices in Natural Healing for Dogs and Cats.* New York: St. Martin's.

Wynn, Susan, and Steve Marsden. 2002. *Manual of Natural Veterinary Medicine: Science and Tradition.* Philadelphia: Mosby.

Rehabilitation Therapy

Bockstahler, Barbara, et al. 2005. *Essential Facts of Physiotherapy in Dogs and Cats.* Ontario: Lifelearn.

Canine Rehabilitation Institute. www.CanineRehabInstitute.com. Partners with Colorado State University; courses are offered year-round in convenient locations across the United States. Offers certification as a Canine Rehabilitation Assistant for veterinary technicians.

Canine Rehabilitation Resource. www.canineequinerehab.com. 1-800-272-2044. Offers general information and a list of educational conferences, including the University of Tennessee program.

Federation of State Boards of Physical Therapy. www.fsbpt.org. 1-703-299-3100.

International Association of Veterinary Rehabilitation and Physical Therapy. www.iavrpt.org.

Levine, David. "Facilities Providing Animal Physical Therapy/Rehabilitation." www.utc.edu/Faculty/David-Levine/Veterinary.HTM#Clinics. 1-423-425-4111. Accessed February 8, 2012.

Mills, Darryl L., et al. 2004. *Canine Rehabilitation & Physical Therapy*. Philadelphia: Elsevier.

Animal Massage

American Massage Therapy Association. www.amtamassage.org. 1-877-905-2700. Lists schools and courses in animal massage.

Colorado Veterinary Medical Association. www.colovma.org. 1-303-318-0447. Designed a course for veterinarians, technicians, and therapists encompassing medical massage for animals. This course allows attendees to be certified in animal massage.

Equissage. www.equissage.com. 1-800-272-2044. One of the longest-established training facilities for massage. Students successfully completing the Equissage program receive 50 hours of continuing education credit, as approved by the National Certification Board for Therapeutic Massage and Bodywork (NCBTMB, www.ncbtmb.org, 1-800-296-0664).

Hourdebaight, Jean-Pierre. 2004. *Canine Massage: A Complete Reference Manual*. Dogwise Publishing.

National Board of Certification for Animal Acupressure & Massage (NBCAAM). www.nbcaam.net. Provides a "Scope of Practice" and "Code of Ethics" for animal massage and acupressure, committee listings, and other resources.

Species Variety: Mice to Tigers

Veterinary technicians may decide to work with less traditional species, from fish and marine mammals to tigers. You may work in a private practice that serves these animals, or you may work for the government, industry, or a nonprofit group. Government agencies—the Fish and Wildlife Service—or marine parks may hire veterinary technicians who learn about marine mammals or fish diseases. Other technicians may focus on exotic animals and work in zoos. All technician programs teach a bit about these species, although the student must usually make an extra effort to learn enough to create a career in that area. This may be accomplished by spending extra time with the course instructor or by taking externships that involve that type of work. An externship is a short-term work-study program required of all veterinary technician students, as outlined by the American Veterinary Medical Association (AVMA).

Pay in the area of "species variety" varies more than any other aspect of veterinary technology, since laboratory animal care falls into the highest pay scale, whereas nonprofit wildlife-care centers may fall into the lowest pay scales (often relying on volunteers). While you are developing your networking contacts, include pay scale as a discussion item, along with other aspects of the career path.

Laboratory Animal Medicine

As Dr. Stacy Pritt, director of Animal Welfare and Regulatory Compliance at Covance Research Products, in Princeton, New Jersey, says, "Vet techs can do a lot more in research than they can in private practice. I supervise a surgical services unit, where three technicians routinely perform surgery. Our activities are governed by federal laws and guidelines, which allow appropriately certified technicians to do a lot more and different types of procedures than are allowed in private practice by state laws. Salaries are good, much better than in private practice."

Daily work

One large area of interest is that of laboratory animal medicine. That includes mice and rats, but also larger animals up to the size of primates. Laboratory animal technicians work in research facilities or universities and often go on to obtain advanced degrees. The work varies with the type of research. Often, the work focuses on just one or a few species (e.g., mice, primates, dogs).

Technicians' skills may be more fully utilized than is sometimes experienced in private practice. Research that involves animals can be controversial because of animal welfare issues. The technician interested in this field must find a work environment that aligns with his or her values.

Sample Job Announcement

Veterinary Technician wanted to function as a member of a team of professionals to provide veterinary care to research animals. The employee will be responsible for inspecting research animals housed by the university and evaluating sick or injured animals; provide routine care such as vaccinations, parasite control, and TB testing; be required to keep detailed and accurate records of health evaluations and surgical procedures; be able to communicate effectively with research personnel and maintain effective working relationships with other personnel. Prior experience preparing animals for surgery and monitoring anesthesia required. Basic data entry skills required. Emergency duties required during adverse weather and/or other emergency situations. Weekend, on-call, and holiday work required occasionally on a rotating basis. Graduate of an accredited AVMA program in veterinary medical technology preferred. Four-year degree or an equivalent combination of training and/or related experience is required.

Qualifications

Laboratory animal technicians can be certified through the American Association for Laboratory Animal Science (AALAS) Certification and Registry Board, which certifies three levels of technician competence: assistant laboratory animal technician, laboratory animal technician, and laboratory animal technologist (AALAS, www.aalas.org, 1-901-754-8620).

Some, but not all, veterinary technician schools teach courses that prepare students to take the AALAS certification exams. Some schools also have externships that can contribute to the work experience needed for the certification exams (six months' experience for the first level of certification). Over the past 45 years, AALAS has certified over 35,000 technicians.

Technicians who are interested in surgery might look into the Academy of Surgical Research, at www.surgicalresearch.org (click on "Certification"). Veterinary technicians often do many surgeries in research after they go through this certification program.

To start
To apply for certification, you will need to fill out forms found on the AALAS Web site, www.aalas.org/certification/tech_cert.aspx. There you will find handbooks, levels of certification, and other study aids.

Aquatic Veterinary Medicine

Whether you're interested in aquarium fish or whales, you can find a job working in aquatic veterinary medicine. Technicians may work with veterinarians in private practice. Fish include fresh- and saltwater aquarium fish as well as the increasingly popular pond koi. Other possibilities include working with a large public aquarium. Aquarists are caretakers of fish, dolphins, and other lower-vertebrae species. Water temperature monitoring, chemistries, testing, and treatment can all be taken care of by skilled veterinary technicians. Demand for these skills is reflected in zoos, pet stores, and public aquariums.

Hillsborough Community College in Tampa, Florida, offers a two-year degree for aquaculture technicians. In an article posted from the University of Florida, Dr. Ruth Francis-Floyd states, "Twenty years ago a career in aquatic animal medicine was not considered a realistic goal because there were so few opportunities. Growth of aquaculture industries, public aquaria, public concern for environmental degradation, use of aquatic organisms in research, and the increased value of aquatic pets have all resulted in a plethora of new career possibilities in this growing and exciting field." She also says this is not a career path for those who are easily deterred. Because this is a growing field, the job opportunities are few and far between at this time.

Technicians wanting to excel as an aquatic caretaker may take this challenge and run with it. Pet owners are increasingly purchasing fish for their home aquariums. The need for husbandry technicians also is growing. Consider water chemistry balance and tank maintenance as an option. Veterinary hospitals offering services for exotic fish would benefit from having a technician who specializes in water testing and fish husbandry.

Wildlife: Zoos and Sanctuaries

You can work with wildlife in sanctuaries, zoos, rescue operations, and private practice.

Zoo work

We've already discussed private practice work, but the following sections cover zoo work, rehabilitation, and sanctuaries.

Daily work

Joel Pond, CVT, executive director of the Association of Zoo Veterinary Technicians (AZVT), has worked in the field for four decades and is also a consultant for Idexx Laboratories. He works at the Lincoln Park Zoo in Chicago, Illinois. He has this to say about zoo medicine:

> My job is similar to others in the field; the species are much different. We work with animals from cockroaches to elephants, marine animals to venomous reptiles. Zoo veterinary technicians perform inhalation and injectable anesthesia on all species, including insects and other invertebrates, fish, reptiles, amphibians, birds, and mammals. These animals may range in size from a few grams to several tons. We perform a large variety of laboratory support in the form of CBCs, blood chemistries, parasitology, urinalysis, cytology, basic blood banking, microbiology, and serology. Other related tasks include take and develop diagnostic radiographs (some use digital equipment); fill and dispense prescriptions; maintain and service all hospital equipment and laboratory apparatus; maintain a high standard of hospital cleanliness; maintain laboratory, medical, and technique logs; interact with the zoo staff (the "client") and zoo public; and give educational talks to keeper staff and colleagues.
>
> As a group we need to be very adaptable and knowledgeable about our animals. We work with venomous creatures from fish to reptiles. We also encounter a higher degree of potentially zoonotic conditions requiring increased biosecurity, especially when working with non-human primates. Veterinary technicians in this field are trained for a variety of emergency situations, which may include veterinary medical problems but also dangerous animal escapes. Many zoo veterinary technicians may also get opportunities to work in field projects around the world.

Technology rapidly changes in zoo animal medicine. Staying abreast of new techniques and newly acquired species in a zoo is challenging. Can you imagine anesthetizing an exotic fish one day and assisting with surgery on an elephant the next? That's diversity! Veterinary technicians working in this field are truly conservationists; sometimes their patients are the last of a species. Joel Pond explains:

> My rewards in this field are many. I am constantly learning something new: about the animals, about medicine, about people, and myself. Working with endangered species, some of which are only alive because of zoos, is immensely rewarding in and of itself. Just adding to the mass of clinical data and normal blood values on previously unknown or rare animals, which may be small, incremental contributions to the science of keeping these animals healthy and alive, is rewarding.

Qualifications

In 1981, 13 veterinary technicians working at zoos throughout the United States decided to create an association for zoo veterinary technicians, which became AZVT, an association that would offer networking and continuing education classes specific to their needs and those of their patients. To begin networking within this group, consider attending one of their annual conferences. The goal of this organization is to improve professional standards, promote continuing education, and contribute to conservation. They offer scholarships and continuing education and provide listings of job openings specific to zoos and of zoos seeking students for externships. You may also consider becoming a zoo specialist. Contact the Academy of Veterinary Zoological Medicine Technicians at www.avzmt.org, not to be confused with AZVT.

If you wish to pursue a career as a zoo veterinary technician, be prepared to put in a number of volunteer hours to gain the needed hands-on experience. Since zoo medicine is so specialized, volunteering at a zoo is the best way to get the needed experience and skill sets. Internships and preceptorships are offered at many zoos. Contact the program director for information about the required vaccinations, housing, and scheduling. Veterinary technician students will enhance their skill levels, and seasoned technicians will enhance their knowledge of anesthesia, treatment, and species-specific diseases.

The North Carolina Zoo is a state-owned and -operated organization. On its Web site, www.nczoo.org, you will find an article about becoming a zookeeper. It states that positions at their zoo are highly rewarding and competitive. On an annual basis, they receive 600–800 applications for zookeepers. A minimum of two years of zoo animal technology and directly related work experience is recommended before applying for a job.

To start

We all enjoy visiting the nearby zoo. Begin networking with the veterinary technicians currently employed by the zoo. Consider asking for a personal tour of the veterinary hospital. Mentioned earlier, volunteering is a great way to get your foot in the door. You may need to create a new position in the zoo's veterinary hospital. Denise Mikita, CVT, stepped into a newly designed position and is the inventory specialist at the Denver Zoo's veterinary hospital.

Sample Job Announcement
(Found on Accredited Zoo and Aquariums Job List)

Wildlife Hospital seeking a qualified candidate for the position of Veterinary Technician. This is a diverse zoological park, home to over 800 animals, with a 320-acre preserve in which numerous species, including chimpanzees, nondomestic hoofstock, lions, and rhinos, roam freely in spacious habitats. Additionally, a variety of avian species, small ruminants, and reptiles are displayed and provide close-up, interactive experiences for visitors. Veterinary Technician's duties include, but are not limited to, the following:

- Providing assistance to the veterinarian in all forms of routine health procedures, field immobilizations, administration of medicine and anesthetics, husbandry, surgery, necropsy, etc.
- Performing in-house laboratory procedures
- Preparing samples to be sent to other laboratories as needed
- Maintaining accurate records, ordering hospital supplies, and inventory
- Caring for and observing animals housed in the Wildlife Hospital as needed, maintaining hospital areas in a clean and orderly condition

Wildlife rehabilitation and sanctuaries

Shawna Finkenbinder, the manager of public relations at the Wild Animal Sanctuary in Keenesburg, Colorado, has this advice for those who want to work at sanctuaries:

> Veterinarians and technicians play an important role in sanctuary operations—yet their previous training in general medicine

only accounts for approximately half of the skills needed. Wildlife medicine, more specifically that relating to large carnivores (which our sanctuary specializes in), requires practical application and internship studies to be proficient. Those seeking careers in this field should plan on obtaining additional hands-on training from or at a facility that directly deals with the species they are interested in.

Sample Job Announcement

Looking for a qualified Veterinary Technician for a sanctuary for elephants, large felids, bears, and other species. The ideal candidate will be a confident self-starter with zoo animal and/or wildlife experience. The current population includes elephants, tigers, and bears, among other species. The Veterinary Technician will be organized and experienced in running an exotic animal clinic. This is a unique opportunity for the right person.

Daily work

Releasing an eagle after rehabilitation is exhilarating and rewarding. Your career may include some rehabilitation within general private practice, but there are also opportunities to make this your full-time focus.

Wildlife Rehabilitation Information Directory, www.tc.umn.edu/~devo0028/, offers a complete list of rehabilitation centers, contact information, and descriptions of animals rehabilitated, as well as credentials of the individuals working there in rehabilitation.

Wildlife rehabilitation centers are located in nearly every state and province. A vast variety of wildlife are rehabilitated, from the exotic albino skunk to the majestic grizzly bear and the blue heron. Alaska has a center, originally a ranch for buffalo and elk, that was transformed into a rehabilitation center after the state began bringing it injured moose. Now the Big Game Alaska Wildlife Center is home to eagles, bears, musk ox, deer, and a variety of game birds.

Another option is becoming licensed to rehabilitate wildlife from home. For instance, a zoo veterinary technician can have a home-care rehabilitation license and also work at the nearby zoo. Wildlife rehabilitation is not about making wild animals into pets. The goal is to relieve the suffering of injured animals—to treat them and return them to the wild. In some instances, injured wildlife are kept in facilities for education purposes. Federal law protects almost all birds; state law protects other kinds of wildlife.

Qualifications

You can work in private practice with veterinarians who hold a wildlife rehabilitation license, or for a nonprofit group. You can also obtain a license yourself. Before rehabilitators are given a license, they must meet special requirements, such as completing training, participating in mentorships, passing facility inspections, and pass oral and written exams. In some cases, permits from the U.S. Fish and Wildlife Service are required. Contact your state wildlife agency to determine the permits, training, and facility you will need. Because jobs with wildlife are generally linked with nonprofit organizations, a solid understanding of not-for-profit management is encouraged. Fundraising, management, husbandry, and knowledge of the wildlife you will be treating are skills needed to properly manage a rehabilitation center.

There is no job description for a rehabilitator other than being extremely flexible. Paid positions will include maintaining the facility, cleaning cages, treating a wide variety of animals, working closely with a veterinarian, supervising volunteers, capturing and transporting injured animals, and providing public education.

The National Wildlife Rehabilitation Association (NWRA) reports that 24 percent of its members are either veterinarians, students, or veterinary technicians. The association members treat hundreds of thousands of injured animals each year, provide educational programs to over eight million people annually, and focus on preserving individual wild animals, rather than preserving an entire species or its habitat. It is the goal of the NWRA to further the education and knowledge of rehabilitators. Since wildlife rehabilitation is relatively new, growing in need and popularity over the last 30 years, the purpose of the organization is to develop high standards of ethics, conduct wildlife care through networking, and foster respect for and protection of wildlife and ecosystems.

Sanctuaries, different from zoos, may also offer you an opportunity to work with exotic animals in a captive setting. Sanctuaries allow exotic animals that previously may have been privately owned to live out their lives in a natural setting. Oftentimes the animals have been purchased illegally and have outgrown or worn out their welcome in a personal residence.

Management of a sanctuary is costly. Fundraising is a large aspect of the work. Animals living in a sanctuary may be "adopted" for a year. This allows the sanctuary to raise funds and awareness. Packages can be bought allowing the donor to receive a certificate of adoption, photos of the precious animal, updates, visits to the sanctuary, and a T-shirt.

To Start

To begin your research in wildlife rehabilitation, you will need to determine state laws. First, identify if you can hold a license in rehabilitation and then move forward. Consider working within a veterinary hospital that includes wildlife rehabilitation, creating your own rehabilitation site (if allowed by law), and working at a sanctuary or rehabilitation center.

Jobs Related to the Environment

Environmental-interest jobs usually involve working with wildlife in a broad sense. Many temporary opportunities arise when human-caused disasters (such as oil spills) require a large number of volunteers.

A group called the Alliance of Veterinarians for the Environment (AVE) encourages veterinarians and nonveterinarians to get involved with careers that have a positive impact on the environment. The AVE is developing a career counseling project aimed at creating a "career-changing tool kit" for individuals wanting to find work related to conservation and environmental health. They will be including information on career paths that require further graduate training, and their career focus targets environment-related work. Topics on its Web site include job openings, climate change, and health.

Leslie Dierhauf, DVM, suggests getting involved in your local community. Volunteering with the local Nature Conservancy group, zoo, or department of natural resources can be a great place to start. Technicians interested in helping others through environmental awareness may find a niche in international work. Government jobs (with the Environmental Protection Agency or Fish and Wildlife Service) might also be appropriate. U.S. Agency for International Development (USAID) fellows also can have a positive impact on the environmental awareness of people in other countries. (See "Government Jobs").

Chapter Resources

Aquatic Medicine

Association of Zoos and Aquariums (AZA). www.aza.org. 1-301-562-0777. Has job listings.

Floyd, Ruth Francis. "Preparing for a Career in Aquatic Animal Medicine." University of Florida, IFAS Extension. Edis.ifas.ufl.edu/pdffiles/VM/VM11100.pdf. Accessed February 8, 2013.

World Aquatic Veterinary Association (WAVA). www.wavma.org. Directories to find veterinarians interested in aquatic animal medicine. Members are veterinarians who work in private practice, academia, government, commercial fish farms, or large public aquariums.

Zoo Work

Academy of Veterinary Zoological Medicine Technicians. www.avzmt.org.

American Association of Zoo Veterinarians (AAZV). www.aazv.org. 1-904-225-3275. Publishes the *Journal of Zoo Medicine* and a list of accredited zoos and aquariums.

Association of Zoo Veterinary Technicians (AZVT). www.azvt.org. 1-312-742-7211.

Association of Zoos and Aquariums. www.aza.org. 1-301-562-0777. Has job listings.

Crosby, Olivia. 2001. "Wild Jobs with Wildlife." *Occupational Outlook Quarterly*, Spring. www.bls.gov/opub/ooq/2001/spring/art01.pdf. Link to information regarding aquatic duties at aquariums and zoo training.

Woodland Park Zoo, Seattle, Washington. 1-206-684-4800. Offers an opportunity for licensed veterinary technicians to volunteer in their Zoo Corps. Other zoos may offer similar opportunities.

Wildlife Rehabilitation

International Wildlife Rehabilitation Council (IWRC). www.iwrc-online.org. 1-408-271-2685. Offers training, continuing education, and networking.

National Wildlife Rehabilitation Association (NWRA). www.nwrawildlife.org. 1-320-230-9920. A professional organization to enhance job experience as a rehabilitator. It offers job listings, educational opportunities, and a complete list of registered veterinarians and licensed wildlife rehabilitators.

Moore, Adele T., and Sally Joosten, eds. 2002. *Principles of Wildlife Rehabilitation*, Second Edition. St. Cloud, MN: National Wildlife Rehabilitators Association. www.nwrawildlife.org.

Environmental Jobs

Alliance of Veterinarians for the Environment. www.aveweb.org/career. Offers volunteer opportunities, advanced degrees, and concentrated courses.

Environmental Care Organization. 1998. *The Complete Guide to Environmental Careers in the 21st Century*. Island Press.

Fasulo, Mike, and Paul Walker. 2007. *Careers in the Environment*. Columbus, OH: McGraw Hill.

Gordon, John, Joyce Berry, and Norman Christensen. 2006. *Environmental Leadership Equals Essential Leadership: Redefining Who Leads and How.* Yale University Press.

National Council for Science and the Environment. www.ncseonline.org. 1-202-530-5810.

The Nature Conservancy. www.tnc.org. 1-703-841-5300.

Starting Your Own Business

Your wheels may already be turning: you want to explore the idea of becoming your own boss and starting your own business. Maybe you have created a widget and feel that every other veterinary technician or hospital will want to buy your widget. Or maybe you have a service you want to provide to veterinary hospitals and you wish to promote your service, such as puppy behavioral classes or integrating new software. Have you considered dog grooming, owning a pet store, or possibly a retail consignment pet store? Following are some very basic guidelines. We strongly encourage you to speak with both an attorney and an accountant once you have identified your initial business plan, vision, mission, and core values.

Starting a Business

No matter what your business, there are two management tools you must know:

1. You must know the technical aspects of your business (e.g., how to make a widget, use computers, or train puppies).
2. You must know how to run your business.

The latter is just as important as the former. The biggest mistake made by new business owners is thinking that their technical expertise will carry them through starting their business. Nothing will lead you to failure faster than that attitude.

For most veterinary technician students, it is in their best interest to first hone technical skills in a practice setting, then expand career options. Thinking outside the box, looking at the big picture, then dividing that vision into manageable pieces can push everyone to the edge of their comfort zone. Go for it!

Once that foundation has been sharpened, follow your passion and expand your ideas. Numerous ideas have already been offered in the previous pages. When you have time to surf the Internet, you will undoubtedly find a treasure trove of ideas. For example, www.bizbuysell.com is a Web site that allows interested parties to view pet-care businesses for sale within each state. A recent search showed a horse-boarding stable for sale in Colorado. Three dog day-care centers were also listed. These were established businesses with a solid client base. A natural pet retailer with a yearly cash flow of $98,000 was selling her business. Oddly paired, somewhat, were an express car wash and an interior dog wash.

Daily work

Depending upon your personal business choice, a large portion of your time will be spent in business management, promotion, financial considerations, and disciplining yourself with time management. Working from home requires more discipline than having a retail store where you must be available for certain hours of the day. Time management is of the utmost importance. Expect to spend one-quarter to one-half of your time with management duties and the remainder of the time doing the actual work for which you are paid.

Self-motivation is critical when you are your own boss. Working without a "monkey on your back" has both up- and downsides. Your success is totally on your shoulders. Generating a vision for your business will help you focus on the important tasks that are both urgent and relevant to your success. Pros include overseeing your own schedule, following passions unavailable in a traditional job, and having the satisfaction of the success being your own. Cons include extreme self-discipline, financial uncertainty, self-doubt about your choice, and overcoming difficult moments victoriously. Reputation and solid business relationships are your highest priorities, offering services that are consistent and valuable.

When you are ready to start your own business, your savings account should be sufficient to sustain you for six to twelve months as you build your business. Pay varies tremendously among individuals and businesses. Adequate savings will tide you over until your business begins to generate adequate income. Realistic, proper budgeting is imperative for both personal and business funds.

Since starting a business is different from being hired as an employee, you can't look up "salary" to determine pay. Your detailed business plan should include market research that will tell you what you can expect to earn for the business as well as how much of that can go into pay for the owner (you).

Qualifications

Before you start your business, be honest with yourself about your abilities. Ask yourself these important questions:

- Are you interested in being your own boss, managing your time, disciplining yourself to work, selling your skills (or your widgets), and tracking down new clients?
- Are you good at record-keeping, or can you hire someone who is?
- Are you willing to study business management and make a business plan?
- Can you personally design a mission, vision, and core values for you and your business?
- What are your start-up costs? What equipment and supplies will you need? What ongoing costs can you project? What will you charge for your products or services?
- How will you target your market and analyze your competition?
- If your work involves travel, will you charge for travel time, travel costs, both, or neither?
- If you'll have an office in your home, is your area zoned for home offices?
- Do you have a good attorney and an accountant who can advise you in legal and tax matters?
- Are you proficient at desktop publishing so that you can create your own brochures, press releases, and other materials? Your start-up budget often won't allow hiring someone for this!
- Who are your potential customers, how will they pay for your products or services, and how will you handle late payments?
- Will you hire employees, and if so, to do what jobs?
- Do you have unrealistic expectations of the personal benefits of being self-employed? You may expect to have more personal time, but chances are that you'll work longer hours than ever before. (This may be offset by far more personal satisfaction with your work and a feeling of greater control of your home life.)
- What kind of insurance will you need? Insurance is not optional. Check with an independent insurance agent who works with other small-business owners. You will need liability coverage, property coverage, and perhaps more. For example, if you use your vehicle for business purposes, you will need additional coverage.
- What business licenses will you need? (See "Chapter Resources.")
- How will you pay your bills during the three to twelve months it will take

to get your business off the ground?
- Can you get a loan to cover your business start-up costs?

Pet Home Care: Pet-Sitting, Pet Walking, and Day Care

Pet home care includes pet-sitting, pet walking, and "doggy day care." Although these services do not require a technician's credentials, technicians are particularly well qualified to fill this niche. For example, although anyone could be a pet-sitter, a technician may have special skills, such as the ability to administer daily at-home medications, which may provide particular benefits for many pet owners. These clients feel reassured that their pet-sitter can monitor their pet for signs of a problem and will be more aware of circumstances when a veterinarian should be called. Remember, your business plan should include market research that will tell you what you can expect to earn for the business as well as how much of that can go into owner pay.

Pet-sitting

Pet-sitting provides an exciting opportunity for veterinary technicians. Owners of multiple pets, exotic pets, and scaredy-cats, as well as those who don't like the thought of their pet in a kennel, will welcome your services.

Daily work

Pet sitters may go to homes to care for pets or even live in a home temporarily. Many pets must be cared for (fed, walked, etc.) at specific times of day. Your workday may include spurts of activity interspersed with sitting around. Time management and attention to scheduling are essential.

Think of new ideas: How about an animal ambulance service (coordinated with local veterinarians), managing pets staying at assisted-living facilities, or tending to K-9 patrol dogs when the officers are on vacation?

You may perform these services as part of your own business, or you may work for a larger business as an employee. These are great work-from-home jobs that can be started with little investment.

A related business is that of cleaning up after pets. Businesses with names such as Scoopy-Poo offer a service picking up pet waste in pet owners' yards. Annual growth of the "pooper scooper" industry is reported at 50 percent in *101 Best Businesses for Pet Lovers*.

As a pet-sitter, you have all the work and all the rewards of running your own business. You must be available when people need pet-sitting, which means working holidays and weekends. Work volume can vary with season, so income may not be consistent.

Pay varies with whether you work for yourself or for someone else and with the volume of work you do. You may already offer your services to clients for pet-sitting. As with most jobs that are done "on the side" or as "moonlighting," you may not be receiving the biggest return for your time if you are not doing this service as an organized business. Many technicians do pet-sitting on a casual basis but have not registered their own business, so they are not reaping the benefits of a business (e.g., business cards, other tax-deductible expenses). Consider establishing a sole proprietorship or limited-liability corporation to reap all the tax benefits and perks you deserve.

Qualifications

Professional pet-sitting has become a career and is one of the fastest-growing entrepreneurial endeavors in the pet-care trade. Pet-sitters are in great demand. There are even professional organizations with detailed Web sites on how to create your business or work for a pet-sitting franchise. How you want to work depends upon your desire to make your personal business succeed. As with other businesses, check with the governing body in your state regarding required contracts, licenses, insurance, and how you perform duties for the client.

To start

Post your business card or flyer on local bulletin boards and at the kennel club. Attend meetings of pet interest groups (e.g., bird fanciers) and pass out your business card. Many state associations allow you to list your business in their directories. For example, veterinary technicians in Colorado who offer pet-sitting and are members in good standing of Colorado Association of Certified Veterinary Technicians (CACVT) can be listed on the association's Web site. They must follow a few guidelines and realize they are representing the profession when they represent themselves as a credentialed veterinary technician offering in-home pet services. This is a free advertisement on the Web site, available as a benefit of belonging to CACVT. Contact your state association for more information. (See guidelines at www.cacvt.com under the "Job Postings" tab.)

Doggy day care

A recent Google search for "Doggy Day Care" came up with 1,480,000 matches! As the human-animal bond increases, so do the services that pamper pets. Offering even pickup and delivery of pets to and from day care is a booming industry that is expected to grow. And if that isn't enough to convince you, *101 Best Businesses for Pet Lovers* says, "The philosophy of doggy day care rests on three fundamental pillars: fun, exercise, and fraternization" (Nigro and Nigro 2007).

Daily work

Doggy day care has numerous benefits for dogs and dog owners, making it a rewarding career choice. Young dogs can be socialized in a safe environment. Potty training is improved because of scheduled breaks. Adolescent pets receive the benefits of exercise and play. Senior dogs are entertained and may even be medicated while at day-care centers. All these benefits create a win/win situation for the dogs and dog owners.

Web sites abound with pictures of dogs swimming in pools, frolicking in a safe, clean environment. Most facilities allow only pets with a good temperament to mingle; rude playmates are not allowed to mix with the masses. Small, short, big, and tall rambunctious dogs of all ages romp around in activities like ball chasing; comforts include shaded patios and plenty of water to drink. Indoor environments show dogs lounging on couches, relaxing on pillows, and resting together. What dog wouldn't be exhausted after a few hours at day care?

Much like day care for children, doggy day-care options are flexible and work around your schedule. You set the hours, and you can choose to make the business as big or as little as you want. However, to get the most business, you must also work around the schedules and needs of the pet owners.

Qualifications

Similar to pet-sitting, be sure to check with your local government agencies to make sure you are in compliance with rules, regulations, and insurance and recognized by the appropriate organizations overseeing day-care facilities.

To start

If doggy day care sounds like a business you wish to explore, there are complete manuals describing the ins and outs of this entrepreneurial opportunity. With over 40 million dog owners in the United States and a large majority of households having no "stay-at-home" person, the demand is huge for this service. With their knowledge of vaccinations, temperament, basic understanding of infectious diseases and disease control, and love for animals, veterinary technicians are great owners of day-care centers.

As with all businesses, be sure to check with your state government to find out what rules and regulations govern doggy day-care centers. There may be state and local laws overseeing this business venture.

Grooming

The grooming business has adopted the human-animal bond approach and is flourishing! Pet grooming tends to the physical needs of the animal and the emotional needs of the pet "parent."

Petgroomer.com stated that the demand for pet groomers would continue to increase. It is estimated there are 4,000 dogs and cats for each groomer. History has shown that this industry seems immune to economic recessions and is estimated to continue growing. The petgroomer.com Web site has everything a person would ever need to begin a business in pet grooming—home-study courses, equipment, promotional materials, magazines, directories, upcoming trade shows, and a list of experienced consultants willing to help you improve your business. It really looks like you can find it all on this one Web site!

Recently a friend adopted a young, sweet, apricot cockapoo. She wrote an email that captures the heart of her puppy's first grooming experience:

> Hey, thought you would enjoy seeing Max after his first haircut. He looked like a fluffy sheep rug before his haircut and now he looks half the size he was before and very COOL (being in Florida). I should have weighed him before his cut. His groomer is called Angel Paws Doggy Day Spa and they lovingly groom only a few dogs daily while playing music, giving them treats, taking them on walks, and holding them in big, cushy crates with nice beds in them. Unbelievable. Max got an A on his first grooming report card (LOL) and she said he was really good for his first cut. He didn't seem stressed at all when I picked him up. YEAH! I got a B for brushing him, so I need to work on that.

Daily work

Groomers may perform their work in a veterinary hospital or at their own business. A large number of veterinary hospitals have a professional groomer, increasing the service base of their business. If you are working in a veterinary clinic, you may be required to be certified in grooming. Being knowledgeable about diseases, skin disorders, and ear infections helps a groomer. If, while performing a grooming procedure, you notice a new bump or infection, you can inform a doctor on the premises, and arrangements can be made for further workups.

When opting to build your own business, as mentioned before, be sure to take the steps to become a bona fide business to reap the benefits of self-employment.

Franchise businesses are also available. Once you do your homework, review business plans, and determine your commitment to the business, purchasing a franchise may be the way to go.

Daily work includes communicating with the pet parent to discuss the needs and outcome of the grooming. Some owners can be very particular! After determining the appropriate clip, the groomer cuts, trims, brushes, shaves, or plucks the animal's fur to achieve the final result. Often the dog or cat is placed on a special table and safely secured. This regulation may differ among states. Many times the pet is bathed, sometimes primped with ribbons and bows, and may even be given a pedicure. Everyone loves it when their pet greets them with a new bandanna at the end of a day spent at the "pet spa"!

Grooming equipment may include shaped, sharp scissors; grooming clippers; nail trimmers; bathing tub; a variety of shampoos; dryer; and brushes. There is also the option of purchasing a mobile unit and going on the road. Vans, trucks, and trailers have well-equipped, spacious work areas. Visit www.petgroomer.com to view industry standards, purchasing options, and advice. Literally a one-stop-shop experience!

Groomers receive both praise and criticism from pet owners, some of whom have particular requirements for their pet's appearance. Sometimes the best way to learn to provide the appropriate grooming for a particular pet is through trial and error. Persistence is the key.

Pet grooming offers a flexible schedule and can provide a good income. If you work in a veterinary hospital, contracts can be set up in numerous ways. The hospital's client base becomes your client base, and referrals to you abound.

Pay

Pay varies with whether you are self-employed or working for another business, and also with the volume of work.

Salaryexpert.com has information about pet grooming. A groomer in Aurora, Colorado, earns an average of $24,000 per year. Simply enter the title "pet groomer" and the zip code you live in, and answer a few questions to receive a customized report.

Qualifications

Groomers must be familiar with the typical cuts desired for or required by every dog breed. They also must be good communicators, since each pet comes with a client with specific needs and emotions. Good relationships with area veterinarians are a plus, since they can refer business to you.

Schools are available with and without certification opportunities. Home study is also an option. It appears that every state has at least one pet-grooming program. Classes can be as short as six months or as long as two years, depending upon your needs. You can find a complete list of schools under the "Schools" tab at www.propetgroomer.com. With your past experience, you may even consider starting a new "pet design" program (high-end grooming) in your area.

To start

There are a number of ways you might pursue a career in pet grooming: attend classes, start your own business, work in an established shop, offer mobile services, or contract with a veterinary hospital. Professional membership associations offer courses and accreditation. Two-year associate's degrees can also be obtained in the field of pet grooming.

Pet Behavior and Training

Training and behavior are often considered together, but they have different meanings. Training refers to teaching "manners," tricks, and basic obedience, as well as special skills ranging from agility to skills required for assistance dogs.

The field of behavior usually focuses on behaviors that have a negative impact on the humans in the pet's life. Of course, there are an association and an overlap between training and behavior. "Behaviorists" may be veterinarian specialists who are board certified in behavior medicine; they are qualified to diagnose disorders that can be treated with behavior modification and various drugs. At the American Veterinary Medical Association national convention in 2008, the National Association of Veterinary Technicians in America Committee on Veterinary Technician Specialties approved the petition for the Academy of Veterinary Behavior Technicians (see "Veterinary Technician Specialties" on page 37). The academy has a Web site, www.avbt.net, offering news, announcements, and candidate and membership information. The "FAQ" tab has answers to many common questions and helpful information.

The pet behavior field has little or no regulation, so anyone can say they work in this area. However, a professional approach is to obtain skills and knowledge beyond "learning as you go." As in the other veterinary technician specialties, documentation of cases, continuing education, teaching advanced courses, and taking an exam enable you to be a technician behavior specialist. Other titles may be misleading and may not truly reflect the competency of the specialist.

Daily work

Dog trainers may offer classes through an association, club, veterinary clinic, or pet store, or they may work on their own. Training may also include animals seen in advertising clips and motion pictures. Therapy dogs offer assistance to physically challenged, hearing-impaired, and sight-impaired individuals. Technicians have helped to train therapy dogs in a variety of arenas.

Working on your own as a pet trainer means you control (and must organize and keep records of) your class schedule and collection of fees. Working through another entity spreads out the work of marketing and record-keeping, so you can focus on the dog training itself. Trainers learn that the object of the training is the dog owner as much as or more than it is the dog; this field could be called "training people to work with their own dogs." Often the owners inadvertently reinforce negative behavior, and they have no clue they are doing it!

A day may consist of morning paperwork, coordinating an upcoming show, midday follow-ups with individual clients, a lunch-'n-learn session at a local veterinary clinic, and an evening puppy class at a nearby Humane Society. Puppy and kitten classes can be held at shelters and may even be a pet-parent requirement. Agility classes, basic behavior, and kitten training 101 programs may be offered to 4-H students, either through an extension office or an animal hospital. Relationships with pet stores, Humane Societies, veterinary associations, and pet lovers are essential for your business to flourish.

Pay

Your wages will vary depending upon the amount of time you dedicate to your pet-training business and how many clients you offer your services to. Researching Florida on www.salaryexpert.com revealed that dog trainers in that state make between $19,000 and $34,000 per year. To search for salaries in your area of choice, enter the title "dog trainer" and your region or zip code, answer a few questions, and you will receive a free document explaining salary.

Qualifications

Technician programs teach basic animal behavior, with courses focusing on dogs, cats, horses, wildlife, and exotics. If you are good at training your own pets, you may think you'd be a good trainer. However, to become a professional, take a professional attitude and pursue legitimate training.

To start

You may start your search viewing Web sites that offer behavior information. If you have been working in the field for a while and are a credentialed veterinary technician, find out what it would take to become a behavior specialist.

One way to begin is by volunteering as an assistant to a local certified dog trainer. Your local dog club is one easy way to meet these people.

A doctor's involvement is necessary for some behavior issues for which pharmacological therapy is required. Dogs and cats may be given medication for syndromes such as extreme anxiety or obsessive-compulsive disorder. Veterinarians may become certified in animal behavior; technicians with a strong interest in this field may seek out these doctors and become a veterinary technician specialist themselves.

Other Areas of Interest

See Chapter 3, "Traditional Veterinary Practice," for a discussion of pet hospice care and alternative/integrative medicine, which includes massage, rehabilitation, and more. All these may be performed under a veterinarian's supervision; some states allow certain aspects to be done by nonveterinarians.

Chapter Resources

See also resources in Chapters 3, 6, 9, and 10.

Biz Resource. www.bizresource.com. 1-604-850-6908.

Business Forum. www.businessforum.com. 1-617-232-6596.

Covello, Joseph, and Brain Hazelgren. 2005. Y*our First Business Plan*, Fifth Edition. Naperville, IL: Sourcebooks.

Edward Lowe Foundation (ELF). www.lowe.org. 1-800-232-5693. Provides information, research, and education experiences that support small-business owners and the free-enterprise system. The foundation provides access to a vast amount of information through online services, computer databases, and publications written for small-business owners. The ELF Web site has a huge list of resources and links to Web sites for all sorts of other business information providers.

Edwards, Paul, et al. 2005. *Home-Based Business for Dummies*, Second Edition. Hoboken, NJ: For Dummies Publishing (a division of Wiley).

Edwards, Paul, Sarah Edwards, and Peter Economy. 2003. *Why Aren't You Your Own Boss? Leaping Over the Obstacles That Stand Between You and Your Dream.* New York: Three Rivers Press, a division of Crown Publishing, Random House.

Entrepreneur. www.entrepreneur.com.

Fishman, Stephen. 2008. *Working for Yourself: Law & Taxes for Independent Contractors, Freelancers & Consultants*. San Francisco: Nolo Press.

Gross, T. Scott. 2004. *Positively Outrageous Service: How to Delight and Astound Your Customers and Win Them for Life*. London: Mastermedia.

In Business. www.inbusinessmagazine.com.

Inc. Magazine. www.inc.com. A great resource for the business owner.

Internal Revenue Service. www.irs.gov. Has important IRS documents for business owners. Most libraries carry copies of all the following documents. If yours does not, write to the Superintendent of Documents, Government Printing Office, Washington, DC 20402; call 800-TAX FORM (800-829-3676); or get documents online at www.irs.ustreas.gov (all documents are free). Handy IRS publications to review include #553, "Highlights of This Year's Tax Changes"; #334, "Tax Guide for Small Businesses"; #535, "Business Expenses"; #583, "Taxpayers Starting a Business"; #587, "Business Use of Your Home"; #917, "Business Use of a Car"; #1200, "List of IRS Publications"; and Form 1040-ES (Estimated Tax for Individuals; includes explanation/worksheet).

National Technological University, Education Center Online. www.ntu.edu. 1-866-688-6797. Offers short courses in business and other subjects.

Nigro, Joseph, and Nicholas Nigro. 2007. *101 Best Businesses for Pet Lovers*. Phoenix, AZ: Sphinx Publishing. Contains much of what you need to know about starting and succeeding in a pet business of your own.

PC World. www.pcworld.com.

Pine, Joseph, and James Gilmore. 1999. *The Experience Economy: Work Is Theater, and Every Business a Stage*. Cambridge MA: Harvard Business School Press.

Small Business Administration (SBA). www.sba.gov. 1-800-368-5855 or 1-800-827-5722. Offers low-cost classes in starting a business and a wide variety of publications that deal with many common questions. Find information at your local public library, or call your local chapter for more information. The SBA Web site has lots of great information, too, with free online courses. SBA loans are also available. The agency rarely loans money itself, but instead backs you with a loan guarantee at the bank. A group called Service Corps of Retired Executives can help you with free advice. Find the nearest group by contacting the SBA or your local Chamber of Commerce.

Smart Business Supersite. www.smartbiz.com. Includes materials to help solve business problems, investigate industries, get trade show information, read about business news, and communicate with other small-business owners. Most full-text material is free; a vast array of book titles and some newsletter subscriptions are available for purchase.

State government. Many states offer services or information for business owners. Call Information in your state capital to get phone numbers. The names of these departments vary slightly from state to state. The state department of taxation and revenue (economic development, board of revenue, etc.) has information about state taxes, business registration/licenses; some state departments have "new business owner" packets of information. The state employment division or employment security has information about unemployment insurance. The state department of labor (labor and industries, workers' compensation department) has information about workers' compensation coverage. The state licensing department has information about state business licenses. Contact your city licensing department for any applicable city business license.

Stephenson, James. 2008. *Ultimate Home-Based Business Handbook: How to Start, Run, and Grow Your Own Profitable Business*, Second Edition. Entrepreneur Press.

Success. www.successmagazine.com.

U.S. Business Advisor. www.business.gov. Gives information about government regulations, publications, and resources for small business. For district office phone numbers, www.sba.gov/localresources/index.html?cm_sp=ExternalLink-_-Federal-_-SBA.

Veterinary Economics and Veterinary Economics Reprint Series (includes *Marketing Your Practice, Charging Fees with Confidence, Starting a Practice*, and more). www.advanstar.com.

Wisenberg, Ronni, with Kate Kelly. 2005. *Organize Yourself!* Third Edition. Wiley. May help decrease paper shuffle, identify strengths and weaknesses in your current routines, and improve overall efficiency.

Pet-Sitting

Brady, Diane, and Christopher Palmeri. 2007. "The Pet Economy: Americans Spend an Astonishing $41 Billion a Year on Their Furry Friends." *Business Week*, August 6.

Duea, Angela W. 2008. *How to Open & Operate a Financially Successful Pet-Sitting Business*. Ocala, FL: Atlantic Publishing Company.

Mangold, Lori, and Scott Mangold. 2005. *The Professional Pet Sitter: Your Guide to Starting and Operating a Successful Service,* Revised Edition. Portland, OR: Pawsitive Press.

Moran, Patti J. 2006. *Pet-Sitting for Profit*, Third Edition. Howell Book House.

National Association of Professional Pet Sitters. www.petsitters.org. 1-856-439-0324. Offers a variety of resources.

Pet Sitters Associates, LLC. www.petsitllc.com. 1-715-831-6004. Offers liability insurance with membership. This site is a "must read" for all interested parties. (Of course, shop around for insurance; your local independent broker may offer competitive rates.)

Pet Sitters International. www.petsits.com. mail@petsits.com. Offers a start-up kit and directory advantage, such that you can list your business on their Web site. This site has a global listing and promotes pet-sitters. Conferences (e.g., about the human-animal bond) and continuing education courses are also provided.

Doggy Day Care

Bennett, Robin K. 2005. *All About Dog Day Care... A Blueprint for Success*. Colorado Springs, CO: American Boarding Kennel Association.

Boutelle, Veronica, and Jean Donaldson. 2007. *How to Run a Dog Business: Putting Your Career Where Your Heart Is*. Wenatchee, WA: Dogwise Publishing.

Dog Day Care Business Plan. www.dogdaycarebusinessplan.com. 1-318-868-7525. Describes a complete business plan.

How to Start a Doggy Day Care. www.howtostartadoggydaycare.com. 1-800-371-1470. Provides forms, releases, business plan, links, and more.

Pet-care Services Association. www.petceteraareservices.org. 1-877-570-7788. A nonprofit trade association for pet-care service businesses. Its members commit to the Pet-care Services Association Code of Ethics and the Pet Owners' Bill of Rights.

Grooming

International Professional Groomers. www.ipgcmg.org.

Kohl, Sam. 2005. *The Business Guide to Pet Grooming*. Hicksville, NY: Aaronco Publishing.

National Dog Groomers Association of America. www.nationaldoggroomers.com. 1-724-962-2711.

Pet Groomer. www.petgroomer.com. Lists books, consultants, help wanted, equipment, and courses.

Pro Pet Groomer. www.propetgroomer.com. A complete list of pet grooming schools by state.

TFH Publications. 1998. *All 87 Breed Dog Grooming for the Beginner*, Second Edition. Neptune, NJ: TFH Publications. Written by a panel of grooming authorities, this book has great, specific instructions.

Behavior and Training

The Academy of Veterinary Behavior Technicians. www.avbt.net. Provides a process by which veterinary technicians may become certified as a Veterinary Technician Specialist (VTS) in the field of behavior.

Aloff, Brenda. 2002. *Aggression in Dogs: Practical Management, Prevention and Behavior Modification*. Wenatchee, WA: Dogwise Publishing.

American College of Veterinary Behaviorists. www.veterinarybehaviorists.org. To find out if there are any board-certified behaviorists in your area.

American Kennel Club. www.akc.org. cgc@akc.com. Offers "Good Citizen" certification of dogs through its Canine Good Citizen Test. This test—rating manners, temperament, socialization, and obedience in real-life situations—was started in 1989. When Fido passes the test, he receives the title "Canine Good Citizen" (CGC). This certification has been used as screening criteria by landlords who wish to rent to a tenant with a dog, by medical facilities wanting therapy dogs, and by shelters to test the adoptability of a dog in their care.

American Veterinary Society of Animal Behavior. www.avsabonline.org.

Association of Pet Dog Trainers. www.APDT.com. 1-800-738-3647. Offers Animal Behavior College to its members at a discount. Includes information about seminars, recommended reading, "Chronicle of the Dog," and a directory of dog trainers.

Certification Council for Professional Dog Trainers (CCPDT). www.ccpdt.org/aboutus .html. 1-212-356-0682. An international testing and certification program. The CCPDT has been certifying pet trainers since 2001, testing biannually at over 700 sites throughout the nation.

Lindsey, Steven R. 2000. *Handbook of Dog Behavior and Training*, Volume 1, *Adaption and Training*. Ames, Iowa State University Press.

Rutherford, Claurice, and David Neal. 2005. *How to Raise a Puppy You Can Live With*, Fourth Edition. Crawford, CO: Alpine Publications.

Society of Veterinary Behavior Technicians. www.svbt.org. A complete list of recommended reading and suggestions on how to build a strong behavioral team within the veterinary hospital for those interested in becoming specialists.

Temp Work: Relief Veterinary Technician

Temp work may be an appropriate line of work for people who like change. Of her job as a relief veterinary technician, Sandy Walsh, RVT, of California says, "My job varies from day to day. One day I may be working in a hospital as a relief surgery technician, the next day I may be meeting with the board of directors as the management consultant for one of my clients, and the next I may be inspecting a hospital for compliance with the veterinary medical board requirements."

Relief Veterinary Technician

A relief veterinary technician is someone who makes a living working a series of temporary jobs (or *locum tenens*, as it is called in human medicine). The relief technician offers services to hospitals for a short-term, temporary "relief" situation. A job may be as short as a half day or as long as several weeks. The reliever can take enough jobs to work full-time, or can work only part-time, as desired.

Daily work

The relief technician keeps a small home office from which jobs are scheduled and where paperwork is completed. A typical month might include working a week at a nearby small-animal clinic; working a weekend at an emergency clinic; and traveling to a nearby small town to work at a mixed practice, staying in a hotel or other housing accommodations. These small-town jobs usually include taking emergency calls during the night.

Relievers do not work regularly at any one clinic. If a veterinary technician works every Monday for ABC Hospital, for example, that technician is a part-time employee, not a relief technician. However, relievers can and do work more than once for any one hospital—for example, the reliever could schedule workdays at ABC Hospital during several continuing education meetings, holidays, and vacations scattered over a year's time.

Relief technicians respond to calls from interested hospitals by first confirming they are available on the requested dates. Then the reliever states his or her fees, and the caller decides whether or not to hire the reliever. The reliever sends a contract or letter that confirms the verbal agreement.

Once on the job, the relief technician steps in where the full-time technician leaves off. For example, if you are filling the shoes of the recovery technician, then your duties will align with his or hers. If you are relieving a large-animal technician, then be prepared to work with horses, cattle, or other ruminants. Relievers walk the tightrope of trying to maintain the clinic's standard policies and procedures and maintaining their own standards of care at the same time.

The amount of travel required for a relief technician depends on the type of work and the size of the community. Relief technicians who live in a large city and limit themselves to small-animal work may not need to travel at all. However, those who live in a rural town may need to travel extensively to get enough work to keep busy full-time.

Relievers who have an unusual skill may also travel more, since hospitals that need those special services are less likely to find someone in their own geographic area. Relievers who are willing to work on large animals, exotics, or birds, or who have skills with anesthesia or dentistry, may find that their services are requested over a wide geographic area.

Relievers assume they will work on weekends, holidays, and during popular continuing education meetings. They plan their vacations at times when others typically don't take theirs, are ready to celebrate holidays on the day before or after the actual date, and plan their own continuing education around other technicians' preferences. Relievers may get more work if they are willing to participate in emergency calls with the on-call doctor. Be sure to discuss this option during initial conversations with the practice manager of the hospital or whoever is overseeing the hiring of independent contractors.

Temp work is not confined to just private practice. Some companies that put on continuing education meetings will hire technicians to fill temporary positions. (See Chapter 7, "Teaching," for details about other work with these continuing education groups.) According to Aine McCarthy, DVM, director of education, North American Veterinary Conference:

> Many technicians work at the NAVC Conference in January and the NAVC Institute in May. They are in full function in our wet

labs, ultrasound, surgery, any and all of the recovery labs, and also in the animal parts labs. They set up, monitor patients under anesthesia and during sedation, and help with the equipment. Our head tech, Debby Sundstrom, is the key coordinator of most aspects related to logistics and staging and all on-site operations. Our technicians are part-time seasonal employees and we rely on them heavily; they are the key to these successful labs.

This career allows for great flexibility and control over personal time and income. The reliever who does a good job and is willing to travel (or who lives in a large city) will have no shortage of work. Disadvantages include travel and working on holidays and weekends. Relievers often have to go to less popular or out-of-area continuing education meetings, since they'll likely have relief jobs during local meetings. Relievers must work with new people all the time—some they may like and some not. The reliever has little control over the clinic atmosphere and policies. As an independent contractor, you may decline further work if you find there is too much conflict with your working style. That is your prerogative as a relief technician.

Pay

The fees charged by relief veterinary technicians vary according to the local economy. Reviewing www.salaryexperts.com will inform you of current charges for specific regions; enter the zip code in the drop-down box. Fees may be charged by the hour or by the day. Remember, you may charge more because you offer a service fulfilling a special need, are covering your own expenses, are paying additional taxes (e.g., self-employment tax), are maintaining your own credentials, and are paying for your own health insurance and uniforms. Most relievers charge a base hourly fee, with a minimum daily fee. Additional fees are charged for mileage to any clinic out of the area, for use of any of your own equipment, for expenses such as hotels, and for taking emergency calls.

Over the long term, relief work can provide a satisfying full-time or part-time career. Relief veterinary technicians sometimes work back-to-back shifts (day clinic/emergency clinic) in order to earn money quickly in the short term (for paying off loans or returning to school).

Relief technicians must realize that they do not receive benefits as a regularly employed technician would—they must take extra care to properly invest and to "sock away" money for insurance and retirement.

Qualifications

Ask the following questions when considering whether you'd like relief work:

- Are you interested in operating your own business and being self-employed?
- Are you comfortable working with people with a variety of personalities? Are you outgoing, personable, and self-assured?
- Do you have enough experience to handle any situation that might arise when you are the only technician on duty? Relief work is not always a good job for a new graduate; the kinds of experiences gained when you are left alone are not necessarily good ones. You must be confident and decisive when working as a relief technician.
- Are you comfortable with any and all anesthetic regimens? Are you able to use a variety of methods, medications, and equipment, or do you prefer one set protocol? Are you comfortable looking up information as needed?
- Are you able and willing to travel? Can you work on holidays and weekends? Are you flexible enough to work different hours each week? Can you take your own vacations at odd times of the year?
- Are you meticulous with record-keeping? Do you write every detail in the patient records?
- Can you write up charges at each clinic according to its policies?
- Are you able to maintain your high standards of practice in spite of your surroundings?
- Are you ready to turn down jobs in clinics where you are not comfortable, even though you need the work? If you take such jobs, are you ready to look the other way?

To start

Many people start doing relief work quite casually. However, to take the full tax advantages of being self-employed, you should go to the trouble of setting up a genuine business. Start by estimating your expenses and establishing your fees and policies. Get a business license (not the same as the veterinary technician credentialing) and write up a contract for every job. Make a plan for marketing your services. Define the mission, vision, and values for your business. Be sure you have enough savings to carry you through your initial slow time, and consult with an independent insurance agent about liability insurance. This is particularly important for veterinary technician specialists doing relief work.

Relief veterinary technicians are different from part-time technicians. A part-time technician is an employee who works a specified number of hours or days at one clinic (regularity is the key, not the number of hours worked). For instance, if you work from 9 a.m. until noon every Monday for ABC Hospital, you are a part-time employee at that practice. You receive a regular paycheck on regular paydays. You may or may not receive benefits, and taxes are taken out of your paycheck by your employer each pay period.

If you are a relief veterinary technician, then you can take certain tax deductions that are allowed for self-employed people. If you are a part-time employee, you should receive benefits that are given to all employees. If you misclassify yourself, then you and the person hiring you may be subject to penalties in the event of an audit.

Agencies

Many relief veterinary technician agencies are springing up across the country. Their services vary from simple matching of relief technicians with job postings to more advanced services that include screening of both the job site and the relief technician. Strongly weigh the pros and cons of teaming with a relief agency. Here are some Web sites that can help you identify such resources:

- www.vetlocums.com
- www.vetrelief.com
- www.vettechrelief.com
- www.vtrs.net
- www.wheretechsconnect.com

Chapter Resources

See also resources in Chapter 5, "Starting Your Own Business."

EnviroVet. www.vetlocums.com.

Glassman, Gary. 2006. "Tax Rules for Relief Veterinarians." *Veterinary Economics*, February. veterinarybusiness.dvm360.com/vetec/Practice+Finances/Tax-rules-for-reliefveterinarians/ArticleStandard/Article/detail/302632.

Rose, Rebecca. 2007. "Have No Fear, Help Is Here." *Veterinary Economics*, April. veterinarybusiness.dvm360.com/vetec/Practice+Tips/Have-no-fear-Help-is-here/ArticleStandard/Article/detail/419449.

Smith, Carin A. 2006. *FlexVet: How to Be One, How to Hire One: The Comprehensive Practice Guide for Relief and Part-Time Veterinarians.* Peshastin, WA: Smith Veterinary Consulting. Includes guidelines for creating contracts for part-time veterinarians.

Smith, Carin, and Rebecca Rose. 2001. *The Relief Veterinary Technician's Manual.* Peshastin, WA: Smith Veterinary Consulting. Includes details about how to set fees, how to get work, tax tips, sample contracts, and more.

Student Advisor Articles. 2006. "Qualities of a Successful Relief Veterinarian." *Veterinary Economics*, April.

State associations. The Colorado Association of Certified Veterinary Technicians, for example, offers a relief page as a benefit to its members. Members can post their service at no charge at www.cacvt.com/jobs. Contact your state's veterinary association to ask about services or information that may help you.

7

Teaching

Technicians know a great deal about a variety of scientific subjects. If you enjoy teaching others, you can get a job teaching at a community college, in a veterinary technician program, or at a veterinary teaching hospital.

Nancy Sheffield, CVT, associate professor, has over 28 years of experience in the veterinary community. She has been teaching for five years and is nearly finished with her master's degree in education. She believes seeing the "lightbulb go off" is the most rewarding part of her job. Nancy enjoys teaching such subject areas as client education and the human-animal bond. She advises, "Learn everything you can, even if you think you will never use it; eventually you will. Be flexible. Be willing. Be positive. Be professional."

The most challenging aspect of her career is finding enough time to do all she wants to do for her students and to create a balanced personal life. Nancy is also active in her state association, working closely with other technicians to create a solid foundation for consistent delivery of rules and regulations for the profession, while sitting on the Colorado Association of Certified Veterinary Technicians Ethics Committee.

Sue Ring deRosset, CVT, is a faculty member in an American Veterinary Medical Association (AVMA)–accredited veterinary technician program at a state community college. She says that her veterinary program director provides a proactive, progressive leadership atmosphere, and she is given autonomy in meeting AVMA criteria. She prepares course structure, syllabi, and PowerPoint presentations; finds guest speakers for the office procedures class; researches lecture topics; and much more.

Both Nancy and Sue serve on college committees, have found their jobs very rewarding, and agree that there is endless paperwork and record-keeping.

College Teaching or Advising

There are many jobs that can be filled by a credentialed veterinary technician that don't require additional training and research. Technicians may be qualified to teach a number of science, anatomy, office management, or animal science courses. They may also be hired as counselors, directors, college retail store administrators, Web site assistants, or internship coordinators.

Daily work

Teaching includes preparing course outlines, materials, and tests; assisting students outside of class time; giving lectures; and staying current on the subject taught. A teacher, as part of the faculty, is often required to participate in various committees and occasionally give a speech to various interest groups.

The counselor's work includes advising students about classes, required experience for graduation, writing resumés and cover letters, conducting mock interviews, and supervising student events.

It's often rewarding to work with students who are interested in and enthusiastic about science or veterinary medicine. As a faculty member, you make great contacts within the teaching community and are paid to expand your knowledge. Cons for those who are "only technicians" include job uncertainty, the political environment at the college, and feeling a bit overshadowed as a technician in an education world. Many jobs are part-time and may not include benefits.

Pay/qualifications

Qualifications and pay vary with the wide variety of positions and levels of funding for each institution. The AVMA oversees all the accredited programs throughout the United States. Requirements for being a teacher are outlined in its accreditation policies and procedures, defined by the AVMA Committee on Veterinary Technician Education and Activities. In that manual, faculty and staff members must teach veterinary technician students in a manner that promotes the role of the veterinary technician and health-care team. The program director can be a licensed veterinarian or a veterinary technician who graduated from an AVMA-accredited program. The institution must evaluate faculty regularly and facilitate professional growth. Teaching may require a teaching credential, although that may be a requirement of the state and not of the AVMA. Each teaching institution can give you information about its own specific requirements, which may vary according to public/private status and other factors.

To start

Teaching positions that are not part of a veterinary technology program will require that you look at specific departments of local community colleges in your area of study (e.g., biology).

Cynthia Medina, MA, has worked in one of the largest veterinary technician programs for over 11 years. As director of Student Services, she finds the most rewarding part of her work is mentoring. "Mentoring students—seeing them bloom under my guidance, encouragement, and calling them on what they need to improve upon to thrive as a professional within the field"—is a key part of her job.

View the AVMA Web site to determine which program will be best for you. Consider location, salary, benefits, etc. There are programs linked with corporations, private institutes, and state colleges. All vary in their approach to teaching and student welfare.

Veterinary Technology Programs

For technicians who love teaching and learning and who won't mind no longer working with animals on a daily basis, veterinary technology programs offer an excellent employment opportunity. There are a variety of positions available within these programs.

Director

The director of a veterinary technician program is in charge of hiring instructors, coordinating the educational program, developing curriculum, proposing and managing a budget, recruiting, interviewing, and counseling students. The director often has teaching duties as well (lectures, laboratories, correcting papers, testing) but spends less time at this than do teachers. Office work, meetings, and telephone time—talking to prospective students and to veterinarians trying to hire technicians who have graduated from the program—are part of the daily work.

Lori Rende-Francis, LVT, professor and director of a community college veterinary technician program in Michigan, first began work as a teacher. After fifteen years of teaching, she became director in 1999, the second veterinary technician to be director of a veterinary technician program. She holds an associate's in applied science, a bachelor's in business administration, and a master's in education. Now, in the twenty-third year of her solid career, Lori still wants to go to work every day. She explains to her students how important it is to be enthusiastic, every morning, about their job. Watching the students gain confidence brings Lori great satisfaction. After students graduate, they often thank her for maintaining such high standards while they were in the program. The community college is very supportive of the veterinary technician classes. Lori is very busy as a mom, wife, and professor and still finds time to be an active member of both the National Association of Veterinary Technicians in America (NAVTA) and the Association of Veterinary Technician Educators (AVTE).

Daily work/pay

The director has two roles: (1) to represent the needs and interests of the program to the administration and (2) to represent the administration's policy and procedures to the faculty and students. Some directors may feel that they have a lot of responsibility and limited authority. Pay is moderate and benefits are good. The job is challenging and full of opportunities to explore new interests and to meet interesting people. Hours are regular and travel isn't required. Veterinarians and technicians who teach or direct are required to maintain their continuing education for credentialing or licensure.

Qualifications

Veterinary technician programs may have different requirements for their director positions. Be sure to view their job postings to determine the qualifications.

To start

Consider having a conversation with the director of the veterinary technician program you graduated from. Network with other teachers and educators to talk about their job satisfaction, schedules, and daily work. You may find that directors and educators are eager to speak with you. They want to see you succeed and are helpful resources.

Educator/teacher

Veterinary technician educators teach a variety of medical and surgical skills to technicians. Many technician programs utilize community veterinarians and technicians part-time for lectures at laboratory sites where students get hands-on experience. Teaching time includes lectures, labs, creating and grading class materials, and paperwork.

Daily work

Veterinary technician educators have less hands-on contact with animals than do those working in private practice, although there is still a significant amount of teaching that involves working with animals (anesthesia, nursing care, radiology labs). Salaries are often comparable to or higher than those of technicians in general practice. Benefits are typically great packages. Rewards include helping students learn and develop, scheduled vacation days, no emergency calls, and teaching subjects that you enjoy and learned in school. Like directors, teachers have to do a certain amount of paperwork and record-keeping.

Qualifications/to start

Some openings are advertised in the *Journal of the American Veterinary Medical Association*, others in the *Chronicle of Higher Education*. Contacting veterinary technician programs may be your best bet; ask about advising and teaching positions.

A background in mixed practice is helpful, since work with all species is taught. Directors need skills in administration, management, and communication. To find job openings, contact the Association of Veterinary Technician Educators and write to the veterinary technician schools that are listed on the AVMA Web site, www.avma.org. The demand is there for more educators, and the number of schools is increasing each year.

Sample Job Announcement (Found in *Chronicle of Higher Education*)

Veterinary technology program—faculty (2 positions) including program director.

Knowledge of current educational methods and strategies; knowledge and experience working on a progressive veterinary team, which includes one or more veterinarians and one or more certified veterinary technicians; and leadership skills necessary for managing a large statewide veterinary technician program are helpful. Applicants are encouraged to apply for one or both veterinary technician program positions. Interviewing for the director position will occur prior to that for the faculty position.

One of the two posted positions must be filled by a veterinarian. DVM/VMD degree from an AVMA-accredited program AND three years of private practice experience where graduate veterinary technicians were utilized OR veterinary technician with an associate degree in veterinary technology from an AVMA-accredited program.

Technicians must also have a bachelor's degree OR a bachelor's degree in veterinary technology from an AVMA-accredited program, AND three years' experience, which includes either three years of private practice experience OR three years instructing veterinary technician students, eligible for certification in Illinois as a certified veterinary technician or, if doctor of veterinary medicine, licensed as a veterinarian in Illinois, or eligible for licensure within six months of employment, and knowledge and diversified work experience including work with live animals in a variety of species within the last three years are required.

Veterinary Assistant Programs

As veterinary technology advances, technician assistants will have a bigger role to play in the veterinary community, and when the demand increases for assistants, so too will demand for teachers of assistants. Efficient service delivery may include well-trained, client-oriented receptionists; credentialed veterinary technicians; technician assistants; and veterinarians. Larger veterinary practices hire people for all these roles. Smaller hospitals may hire fewer people to fill fewer slots. (See Chapter 1, "Preparing to Enter the Job Market," for a description of the different roles.)

Pima Community College is one of many that offers both technician assistant and veterinary technician courses. There are fundamental differences between the two jobs, so be sure you understand the courses you will be teaching.

Both part-time and full-time positions are available for technicians who want to teach. With the projected increase of technicians in the United States estimated at 41 percent by 2017, there will be a demand for teachers of both technicians and technician assistants.

Working With Veterinary Continuing Education

Continuing education meetings for veterinarians have evolved from lectures to hands-on learning. With that change have come many opportunities for volunteer, part-time, or full-time work for technicians. They may participate in the primary role of "technician," caring for animals used in teaching labs, assisting with anesthesia, and so on. They may participate as educators. They also may work for one of the many companies that conduct veterinary training. This is a business that is growing, with many players such as the North American Veterinary Conference, Western Veterinary Conference, Central Veterinary Conference (with meetings on both coasts and in Kansas City), and many more. See Chapter 6, "Temp Work: Relief Veterinary Technician," for details about temporary jobs with continuing education meetings.

Ramona Weisenberger, RVT, has this to say about her jobs working for two different organizations in Las Vegas, Nevada:

> My title is bioskills laboratory manager and I am employed by the Western Veterinary Conference and the Oquendo Center for Clinical Education in Las Vegas. The Oquendo Center is a 66,000-square-foot teaching facility. The Western Veterinary Conference, which takes place in Las Vegas every February, is one

of the largest providers of continuing education for veterinarians, veterinary technicians, and practice managers in the country.

As the bioskills laboratory manager, my job description is long and varied and I am fairly certain quite different from the "norm" for veterinary technicians. I am responsible for course content, recruiting lab instructors, securing equipment and/or supply sponsorship, technical staffing, animal care and use, and the orchestration and execution of all of our annual conference laboratory offerings.

I am equally responsible for the same duties for the course offerings in the Oquendo Center for Clinical Education, where we will provide opportunities for veterinarians, veterinary technicians, and practice managers to attend courses throughout the year. The courses will be hands-on learning experiences lasting several days rather than just the typical 4 or 8 hours offered during most conferences, providing the attendees with much more opportunity for proficiency and confidence after each lab experience.

The most challenging aspect of my career at times is working with an overwhelming number of administrative personnel who have no medical, laboratory, or technical knowledge and have no understanding of what technicians do.

Chapter Resources

See also resources in Chapter 15, "Government Jobs" (with any agency, you can become a teacher of the skills you learn on the job, teaching other people new to the agency) and government jobs with the extension service (extension agents' jobs are as educators).

American Association of Veterinary State Boards (AAVSB). www.aavsb.org. 1-877-698-8482. Oversees the testing of veterinary technicians and offers support to the groups regulating the profession. There are two veterinary technician program administrators. Contact them for questions regarding taking the test, transferring test scores, or test reviews.

American Veterinary Medical Association (AVMA). www.avma.org. Advertises veterinary technician teacher openings through the AVMA Career Development Center's Job Placement Service. A complete list of veterinary technology programs accredited by the AVMA in the United States can be found on the Web site.

Association of Veterinary Technician Educators (AVTE). www.avte.net. Holds a three-day symposium every two years in the summer at different sites, providing the opportunity to bring together the veterinary technician educators from North America. Subjects of talks include information for program directors (recruitment, finances), educators (teaching tips, distance education), and other pertinent issues. Attendance averages 100–300 individuals. This is a good place to network, make contacts for potential jobs, and find out what work is really like. AVTE produces a quarterly newsletter that includes job announcements and information about new veterinary technician programs at various colleges.

Chronicle of Higher Education. www.chronicle.com. 1-202-452-1033. Includes meetings, seminars, workshops, and classified employment advertising for teachers and higher education administrators.

Committee on Veterinary Technician Educators and Activities of the AVMA. www.avma.org/About/Governance/Councils/Pages/Committee-on-Veterinary -Technician-Education-and-Activities-Entity-Description.aspx. Composed of 19 members—veterinarians, technicians, and public members—all with varying backgrounds and specialties. Meetings are held twice a year in Schaumburg, Illinois.

DVM Newsmagazine panel. 2007. "Examining the Roles of Veterinary Technicians." *DVM Newsmagazine*, July 1. Lengthy article; however, it is vital for technicians to know what is being discussed by the experts and the obstacles ahead of us. veterinarynews.dvm360.com/dvm/Examining-the-role-of-veterinary-technicians /ArticleStandard/Article/detail/446523.

Pima Medical Institute of Veterinary Assistants. www.pima.edu. 1-520-206-4500. Offers Pima technician assistant programs. Programs may be found through Pima institutes around the United States.

Raffel, Teri. 2007. "In the News for Members." *NAVTA Journal*, Winter. Synopsis of the gathering of veterinarians and technicians at the DVM Newsmaker Summit 2007.

Raffel, Teri. 2007. "VTTC Meets." *NAVTA Journal*, Winter.

Veterinary Technician Testing Committee (VTTC). Meets annually to review and refine the Veterinary Technician National Exam (VTNE). The committee is composed of 14 members who are veterinarians and technicians from the United States and Canada. A committee of the American Association of Veterinary State Boards.

Practice Management

Practice management is a natural progression for a number of technicians. Some technicians steer away from the job as if it were the plague, while others embrace the challenges of human resources, enjoy creating financial reports and building team efficiency, and wish to seek education in practice management. Those who are drawn to this profession often take the "manager's motto" to heart: None of us is as smart as all of us.

Some veterinary technicians blame veterinarians' lack of business understanding for technicians' underutilization and relatively poor pay. Stronger focus must be placed on practice management, with attention to team development and satisfaction, good wages, and a clear practice philosophy and vision. Technicians working with good managers will experience more job satisfaction.

Both leadership and management are needed. Leaders understand the big picture, defining where the clinic is going; this is often called the vision. Managers oversee the tasks and take care of the nitty-gritty, day-to-day duties to get there; this is reflected in the mission.

Katherine Dobbs, RVT, CVPM, began her management career as a client services technician, then worked as a director of client services, and is now a certified veterinary practice manager. "I started by helping with various management duties while still working in client services. First, I performed smaller tasks, like employee scheduling, and then moved up to more complex tasks, such as interviewing and hiring staff. Eventually I was made senior manager of the client services staff. When the front office supervisor left the practice, I took a full-time management position to oversee the client services staff and the receptionists," she explains. She really moved up the ladder. "The compassion I felt toward our clients transitioned into a desire to make the work meaningful to the staff. This made me realize that I should pursue a career in management. When I worked full-time while attending tech school, I never would have imagined that a management career would be in my future. Now, I can think of nothing more fulfilling."

Mary Berg, BS, RVT, RLATG, VTS (Dentistry), was hired because of her administrative background to be the practice manager at Gentle Care Animal Hospital. Along with the day-to-day activities of managing a three-doctor practice, Mary has taken her dental specialty test, fulfilled the requirements established by the academy, and is certified as a veterinary technician specialist in dentistry. With that added expertise, she is their veterinary dental specialist. She trains the staff to perform dental procedures properly and to give quality home-care instructions. She enjoys educating both clients and team members on the benefits of good dental care for pets. Hiring, firing, employee relations, and payroll are her least favorite tasks.

Published in 2012, *In the Middle: A Head Technician's Guide to All Things Middle Management* by Kelly Lynn Cronin, BS, LVT, RVT, is a fantastic resource for veterinary technicians heading toward or already performing head technician duties. The book is full of antidotes to the challenges a veterinary technician experiences as she or he transitions into middle management. It also includes examples of duties, obstacles, solutions, and forms.

Kelly has this to say about making the transition to management:

> The traditional way technicians become head technicians is through working hard and being exceptional technicians. There are certainly examples of head technicians who perhaps got to their position by way of friendships or seniority, but I venture to guess they are few and far between. One of the biggest problems with [growing into a management role without adequate training] is that, because most head technicians are exceptional technicians elevated to a role of management, there are occasions when a head technician's management expertise is lacking compared to their technical abilities.

Types of Management: Administrator to Office Manager

When searching for a job as a practice manager, consider the three categories defined by the Veterinary Hospital Managers Association (VHMA): hospital administrator, practice manager, and office manager. Different titles have different levels of responsibility; samples of the job descriptions can be found on the VHMA Web site (www.vhma.org) under "Sample Document Library."

The *hospital administrator* works under the direction and supervision of the practice owner(s). The administrator oversees human resources, finance, marketing, and operations. This person is responsible for the overall operation of the organization, as well as for activities that relate to the future growth of the organization (e.g., strategic planning and marketing).

The *practice manager* works under the direction and supervision of the practice owner(s) and/or hospital administrator. This person makes most of the day-to-day management decisions, including financial, inventory, marketing, personnel, and facility-management ones.

The *office manager* works under the direction and supervision of the practice owner(s) and/or the practice manager. This person is responsible for training and supervising the front-office staff, establishing protocols for scheduling appointments, managing the client/patient database, processing clients' payments, and handling customer relations.

The *head technician* or technician manager performs the same duties as the technician and supervises the technical staff.

Daily work

Daily work varies greatly among hospitals. As with any job application, it is best to review the job description before your interview. Management duties at one hospital may be much different from those at a hospital across town. For the most part, managers oversee human resources (HR) duties, including scheduling, holding staff meetings, evaluating employee performance, hiring and discharging employees, and resolving any grievances. Reviewing or developing job descriptions, employee handbooks, and policies and procedures is another HR responsibily.

Financial duties include budgeting, computer input of expenses, reconciling accounts, paying bills, inventory management, monthly collections, credit management, payroll, taxes, and working closely with the accountant.

Communication may include team newsletters and frequent in-house staff training. Client communications may include consent forms, after-surgery home-care instructions, Web site information, health-care reminders, and client newsletters. Results of client surveys, focus groups, and referrals will also be directed to the manager. Welcome letters, thank-you-for-referring notes, and pet birthday cards are greatly appreciated and improve the bond between pet owners and the hospital. Understanding pet health insurance will prove to be an asset. Delegating preparation of kitten and puppy kits and senior wellness packs, equipment maintenance, accurate counting of controlled drugs, and client callbacks are important aspects of a manager's job. Delegating hospital tasks to dependable, loyal, trustworthy team members will enable the manager to focus on other duties.

Computer work plays a big part in daily work. Overseeing charges, laboratory reports, and self-audits are all extremely relevant to the success of the hospital.

More and more veterinarians are convinced that it is in their best interest to hire a practice manager. The first step is for the owner to define the position and scope of responsibilities and authority. Managers and owners must be aligned in their philosophy and vision. Conflict may arise when communications fail and job descriptions are undefined. The most challenging aspect is when a manager is hired, then not given the authority or support to do the job properly.

There are days managers want to pull their hair out. Then there are days that they feel appreciated and respected. Respect and appreciation are a two-way street. Empathy goes a long way in achieving your goals as a manager. Seeking first to understand, then to be understood, at times is challenging for people in a managerial role. The "one-minute manager's" symbol—a one-minute readout from the face of a modern digital watch—is intended to "remind each of us to take a minute out of our day to look into the faces of the people we manage and to realize that they are the most important resources" (Blanchard and Johnson 2001).

Some technicians who excel at their work are promoted to a management position, only to find they don't like the work. Being an excellent technician is totally different from being a manager. For a manager, there is less animal contact; your work changes from being task-focused to being people-focused. Instead of performing medical procedures, you help others do so. You can't always be "friends" with everyone. Yet you are rewarded by seeing others learn and excel, watching them become proficient in their work just as you were.

Pay

Pay varies widely, depending on the area of the country and the supply and demand. The 2009 *VHMA Survey of Compensation for Hospital Managers* showed these averages:

Office Manager	$36,000 per year
Practice Manager	$45,000 per year
Hospital Administrator	$60,000 per year

The American Animal Hospital Association's *Compensation and Benefits Review*, Seventh Edition (based on 2011 data), shows these averages (rounded numbers; some reported as hourly wages and others as annual salaries):

Receptionist Manager	$13.38 per hour
Technician Manager	$16.95 per hour

Office Manager	$15.51 per hour
Practice Manager	$44,236 per year
Hospital Administrator	$60,330 per year

Qualifications

There are no state regulations on qualifications for management of a veterinary hospital. For any position, computer skills are essential. Overseeing charges, laboratory reports, and self-audits is all extremely relevant to the success of the hospital.

Basic knowledge of QuickBooks or Quicken software programs is advantageous. Certification is available in both Microsoft and QuickBooks. Visit their Web sites to view options for training, online classes, and exams. Most classes are self-paced and offer options for certification.

"There are literally dozens of different types of Microsoft certifications. So, depending on what a technician is doing, they might consider how that would help a practice. Hardware certification helps if you work on networks; they have software certification for Internet or business (Office, Outlook, Front Page, etc.). Many clinics struggle with integrating technology into their practice—both hardware and software. There is a big opportunity for someone who understands the technology and how practices operate," states Sheila Grosdidier, RVT. She has a certification in Microsoft hardware, allowing her to assist veterinary hospitals in a number of ways.

Other qualifications include the ability to multitask, prioritize, organize, and delegate. Conflict resolution skills are mandatory. Empathy ranks high as a desired trait. Active listening skills are a must.

You can become a certified veterinary practice manager (CVPM) to increase the number of your potential jobs and your pay. CVPMs receive their certification through the VHMA. The CVPM program is accredited by the National Commission for Certifying Agencies. Requirements for testing can be found on its Web site (www.vhma.org). Certification courses may be completed online through St. Petersburg College (www.spcollege.edu). The program assists students and managers in qualifying for the VHMA examination for certified veterinary practice managers.

The VHMA publishes a monthly newsletter and holds an annual meeting that includes educational courses; some state chapters also hold educational meetings. VHMA membership benefits include access to salary comparisons, focus studies, a career center, benchmark surveys, and much more.

Classes in management may be attended at most major veterinary conferences, at both state and national levels. The American Animal Hospital Association (AAHA) and many consulting groups provide management classes or training, ranging from one day to weeklong presentations. Consultants also offer on-site training tailored to the needs of the manager and the practice.

Sample Job Announcement *(Found on the JuJu Web site)*

Experienced FT Hospital Manager wanted for small animal/exotics practice in Yavapai County, AZ. Supervisor/management, training, budgeting experience preferred. Must be a motivated self-starter with experience in the veterinary setting. Excellent competitive salary with comprehensive benefits. Supportive work environment.

Sample Job Announcement *(Found on WhereTechsConnect.com)*

Animal Hospital is seeking a Technical Supervisor to join our dedicated team. The selected candidate should have 2 years of experience as a veterinary technician, as well as experience in a supervisory or managerial role. We are looking for a strong leader for our technicians and a managerial partner for our Medical Director and Office Manager. Responsibilities include: hiring, training and supervision of all technical staff, medical purchasing, as well as technical responsibilities within the hospital. We are a high-energy, fast-paced hospital with a great team. We offer competitive wages, medical/dental/vision, 401(k), generous pet-care discounts, and more! We offer a competitive salary commensurate with experience for the right candidate.

To start

Many veterinary managers are promoted from within, becoming managers of the hospitals in which they work as technicians. They may first become the "head technician" and then move to greater responsibilities for the entire clinic. To prepare for these positions, it is important to take courses in management and not just assume you can learn management on the job. Being an excellent technician does not teach you how to be an excellent manager.

If you have taken courses and are qualified as a manager, you can view the job Web sites (see resources in previous chapters) for job openings.

AAHA has collaborated with My Veterinary Career to create a powerful resource for veterinary technicians and managers. On their site for job openings, www.myveterinarycareer.com/Visitor/JobOpenings.aspx, you will be able to search for various positions throughout the nation. Other services provided include résumé building, matchmaking, and a multiscreening process.

VetMgrCentral is a company that has matched practice managers and veterinary hospitals across the United States and Canada. The company began assisting veterinarians with management services in 1989. Links included on its Web site, www.vetmgrcentral.com, will help you find more veterinary manager associations, recommended reading, resources, and veterinary management education.

Chapter Resources

American Animal Hospital Association. www.aahanet.org. 1-800-252-2442.

American Veterinary Medical Law Association. www.avmla.org. 1-312-233-2760. You do not have to be a lawyer to attend their meetings (held at each annual AVMA meeting) or join their group.

Blanchard, Kenneth, and Spencer Johnson. 2001. *One-Minute Manager*. New York: Berkley Books.

Blanchard, Kenneth, and Robert Lorber. 2001. *Putting the One-Minute Manager to Work*. New York: Berkley Books.

Brice, Carleen. 2011. "Compensation and Benefits: Who Is Making More and Who Is Making Less?" *Trends magazine*, January/February.

Certification in QuickBooks. quickbooks.intuit.com/product/training/certified_user _program.jsp. Online class with exam.

Cronin, Kelly Lynn. 2012. *In the Middle: A Head Technician's Guide to All Things Middle Management*. Raleigh, NC: Lulu Press.

Donovan, L. 2007. "Connecting with Clients: A Talk with Katherine Dobbs, RVT, CVPM." *Veterinary Technician Journal*, October.

Grosdidier, Sheila. 2007. "Coach Your Boss." *Firstline*, September/October.

Hawkins, David. 2003. "Defining the Relationship: The First Step Is Commitment." *Trends magazine*.

Heinke, Marsha L., and John B. McCarthy. 2012. *Practice Made Perfect: A Complete Guide to Veterinary Practice Management*, Second Edition. Lakewood, CO: AAHA Press.

Levoy, Bob. 2007. "The Rules of Retention." *Veterinary Economics*, October.

Microsoft Certification. www.microsoft.com/learning/mcp/mcdst/requirements .mspx. Lists exams and electronic learning; view site to determine which email to use to direct inquiries.

My Veterinary Career, powered by AAHA. www.MyVeterinaryCareer.com. Matchmaking veterinary service assisting veterinary professionals looking for open positions and hospitals looking for candidates by placing people based on hospital culture and needs.

Smith, Carin. 2008. *Team Satisfaction Pays: Organizational Development for Practice Success.* Peshastin, WA: Smith Veterinary Consulting. Contains a specific outline for team development, hospital structure, and management. Includes a CD with team exercises.

Smith, Sally B., and Margi Sirois. 2004. "Practice Management." In *Principles and Practice of Veterinary Technology*, Second Edition. Philadelphia: Mosby.

Society for Human Resource Management (SHRM). www.shrm.org. 1-800-283-7476. Provides a wealth of information, articles, and continuing education.

Stratman, Susan C. 2003. "Where Does All the Money Go?" *Veterinary Technician Journal*, July.

Veterinary Hospital Managers Association (VHMA). www.vhma.org. 1-817-599-2702.

Consulting

Sheila Grosdidier, RVT, recently became a partner in a consulting firm. She has been in the veterinary profession since 1982. She has an associate's degree in veterinary technology, a bachelor's degree in behavioral sciences, and is Microsoft-certified in networks and hardware. Her role as a consultant is to work with veterinary practices to implement a business plan to achieve their goals. She also presents at various conferences, publishes articles, and looks for opportunities to give back to the profession. Sheila's advice: "Don't be limited by your thoughts; know that this profession can offer you all the enjoyment, satisfaction, and fulfillment you want in a career. I love feeling like I am making a difference in the lives of pets and in the lives of team members."

Consulting

A consultant is someone who charges a fee to share special knowledge and to give specific help or advice to a client. The advice can be in the area of business, career coaching, technology, computers, management, or just about anything else.

Consultants are hired for assistance in a specific problem area (which can be broad or narrow) for a specified length of time (which can range from weeks to years). A consultant is a combination of teacher, leader, and mentor who leaves each client with solutions and new ideas that can be put into practice long after the consultant has gone.

Technicians can work as consultants for businesses ranging from veterinary clinics to livestock feed companies. For instance, one technician with an extensive background is hired by shelters to train their employees.

VetPartners, an association of veterinary consultants, has veterinary technicians as members. These technicians have taken their career to new consultant heights.

Daily work

Consultants can work on their own or as part of a team. They usually travel frequently, since they are most effective when they have seen and evaluated their client's environment.

On-site visits are preceded by background study and are followed by telephone consultations. Before an on-site visit, the consultant obtains as much information as possible about the client to maximize use of time during the visit. The consultant's office work may include studying demographics; writing materials such as office manuals, contracts, and client educational materials; analyzing financial, medical, or nutritional data; writing articles and speeches; developing ideas for seminars, then marketing and planning the specifics for those seminars; and keeping up with new developments in the consultant's area of expertise.

Some consultants work as trainers, conducting workshops that are targeted at a specific skill set. Examples include training in communication, giving feedback, creating job descriptions, and leadership skills.

Technician consultants may be hired by any of the following:
- Veterinarians and veterinary hospitals
- Veterinary medical equipment companies
- Veterinary computer software companies
- Pharmaceutical companies
- Attorneys

The consultant working solo has a small office that may be in the home. This work space requires a computer, telephone, answering machine (voice mail), and copy/fax machine. A cellular phone helps the consultant keep in touch with clients while on the road.

Consultants frequently use computer programs to analyze data, to communicate with clients via electronic mail, and to keep their own business records. Consultants have to market their own business, too, which is done by word of mouth and advertising, including creating advertisements or announcements for direct-mail solicitation or for use on the Internet. They also go to meetings that are likely to be attended by potential clients, to meet people and spread the word about their services (veterinary, product, equipment, and trade shows). Consultants often have a Web site to promote their services.

Most consultants are regular speakers at veterinary, technician, and related industry meetings. Speaking engagements let potential clients evaluate the consultant's expertise as well as educate the audience. Many consultants also create their own seminars, which they offer independently from other veterinary-related meetings. Clients may attend these seminars as a way to pick up business tips and then may decide to hire the consultant for specific help.

Consultants also publish regularly in journals or magazines appropriate to their area of expertise (e.g., business consultants might write for *Veterinary Economics* magazine, and technician utilization consultants might write for *Firstline*). Writing is done to gain exposure, to disseminate word about their work, to establish their credentials, and to educate potential clients about the benefits or need for their services.

The work of a consultant involves travel, which could be a pro or a con for individuals, but helping others make positive change is rewarding work.

The consultant initially often causes clients to be dissatisfied—by pointing out problems and by creating change—before they are satisfied. The consultant must differentiate between what the clients want and what they need. Consultants may carry a large accounts receivable, so collecting payment is a constant job. Soliciting new clients is an everyday need (direct mail, attending meetings that potential clients might attend, public speaking, etc.). Some clients may become "management junkies," who revolve through a series of consultants without making any positive changes. Working with such clients can be frustrating. Other clients don't take the advice given and thus don't see any benefit.

Consultants who work alone may work long hours and get little time off. Their businesses consist of no product, just a service based solely on their own work. It may be difficult to build equity and create a saleable business—they have little or nothing at retirement. Like other self-employed people, they must concentrate on creating a good retirement fund and manage their money wisely.

Pay

Consultant fees vary depending upon the service provided. You may set an hourly fee or a daily charge. More is charged for giving seminars, which require extensive preparation. Hourly fees may be broken down into increments (1 minute, 15 minutes, etc.), and variations of fee structures are common (e.g., fee per month, fee for basic job plus hourly fee). Remember that not all work time is billable time. Marketing, office record-keeping, studying (when not for a specific client), preparing speeches, and some travel are done on your own time and at your own cost. Clients tend to prefer a basic fee with administrative costs included, rather than a bill with all kinds of extra little charges added for phone, copying, etc.

Management consultants may work for a client on a short-term basis (a few days, weeks, or months); they may be hired for a year at a time, to help with long-range projects; or they may be hired for repeated management services, helping with bookkeeping, accounting, or human resource management.

Qualifications

Consultants are problem solvers who make a living helping people do things better, faster, cheaper, and easier. Consultants must travel frequently, be comfortable speaking in public, stay cheerful and positive with every client, be flexible, and enjoy working with and helping a wide variety of people.

Writing skills are necessary. All verbal recommendations must be followed up in writing. Consultants often produce newsletters for their clients. They spend a lot of time on the telephone and with electronic correspondence.

Speaking skills are a bonus. Speaking serves to educate and also to self-promote. Without any "advertising," your presentation, by itself, promotes you as a consultant. Join Toastmasters to become proficient in public speaking. (See "Chapter Resources.")

Consultants are team leaders. They must continually come up with new solutions for new problems, easily changing their approach for different clients.

Consultants need to be able to put a dollar-benefit value on the advice they give. They must be able to show with numbers that their fee will be recouped in higher profits for the client. The hospital wants to see a return on its investment (ROI). As consultant Mark Opperman states, "Cost is only an issue in the absence of value."

Consultants must have a great deal more experience and breadth of knowledge than their clients. However, they need not know everything about everything. Many consultants have depth of knowledge in one focused area, such as financial management or human resources.

Specific skills are required as well as technical or subject knowledge. In addition to excellent writing and speaking skills, they must be great communicators and be able to interact with all kinds of personalities. They must be knowledgeable about human behavior, needs, and desires and be effective at motivating people to work together as a team. They must understand fear of change and how to help their clients overcome that fear with positive results. Computer skills are essential (at a minimum, the ability to use a variety of software programs and online services; at a higher level, the ability to tailor specific software to a client's needs). Many consultants obtain additional training to aid in the business aspects of consulting. Consultants also must be comfortable leading, working alone, selling their skills, and attracting new clients.

To start

Consultants can be self-employed or work for a company; they may work alone or as part of a team.

A consultant's expertise can be gained through work experience. Being really good at your work in only one hospital is not sufficient; every hospital is different. If possible, gain experience in practices of all sizes, with different management structures (relief work is one way to get a look at many practices).

One way to gather more experience on your path to consulting work is to take a job with the government or in industry. That way you get paid for your time and you learn along the way. Take the opportunity to work on a variety of career paths, even those you may not like, in order to broaden your background and knowledge. See Chapters 12–15 for more details.

Another route to acquiring expertise is to take classes or gain an advanced degree (in business, finance, human resource management, economics, health-care administration, or agribusiness). You needn't worry about leaving your job to go back to school. More and more universities are offering short-term intensive courses, correspondence courses, or online courses. Others have branch and evening programs targeted at people who are employed full-time. You can take courses with or without the intention of getting a degree. Look for courses that involve "action learning," which includes skills practice and not just reading books or attending lectures.

Many consultants have a background in management, with a certificate in veterinary practice management or a professional certification or degree in human resource management. (See Chapter 8, "Practice Management," for details.)

VetPartners is an association for consultants. Members include veterinarians, technicians, attorneys, accountants, marketing specialists, human resource managers, financial managers, and people with a variety of other interests. What they all have in common is that they are consultants to the veterinary profession. Joining this group will help you network with other consultants and learn more about this career option.

Types of consulting

There are two main kinds of consultants: business consultants and industry consultants, and the work is quite different.

Business consultant

Business consultants evaluate the internal operations of a veterinary clinic or other business and assist the owners in areas of weakness. They work with business owners or managers to improve the performance, profitability, and goals of the company.

Assistance may be offered in the following areas:

- Improving team efficiency
- Evaluating staff pay and benefits
- Managing time effectively
- Ensuring compliance with Occupational Safety and Health Administration regulations
- Improving competence of doctors (in medicine or surgery) or staff (technical or receptionist duties)
- Developing a new practice, from acquiring bank loans and hiring building contractors to preparing for an open house
- Moving to a new location or planning a new facility
- Improving paperwork (medical records, contracts, hospital manual)
- Targeting new clients or preparing a marketing blitz
- Monitoring income and expenses
- Preparing a marketing plan
- Reducing taxes, using correct tax forms, and keeping up with changes in tax law
- Installing, updating, and improving the use of computers and software
- Creating custom software for the business
- Assisting with partnership negotiations or sale of a practice
- Planning for the future

Industry consultant

An industry consultant assists companies by the following:

- Presenting or teaching technical information to the company's clients or staff
- Tracing the source of poor product performance in the field
- Evaluating the reason for equipment failure
- Evaluating and reducing costs of doing business
- Providing technical assistance to attorneys working for clients involved in a lawsuit

Industry consultants are likely to find work in small companies that do not need or cannot afford to have someone on staff full-time to fill intermittent needs, or they work for larger companies when specific expertise is temporarily needed in areas that those companies don't usually handle.

Chapter Resources

See also resources in Chapters 3, 6, 9, and 10.

AAHA Veterinary Management Institute. https://www.aahanet.org/education/VMI.aspx. 1-800-883-6301. Offers a comprehensive, "mini-MBA" program designed specifically for veterinary professionals by the American Animal Hospital Association and Purdue University.

Academy of Veterinary Consultants (AVC). www.avc-beef.org. 1-913-766-4373. An association of veterinarians involved in beef cattle medicine, herd-health programs, and consultation.

Altman, Rick. 2007. *Why Most PowerPoint Presentations Suck*. Boston: Harvest Books, a division of Houghton Mifflin Harcourt.

American Veterinary Health Information Management Association. www.avhima.org. 1-662-325-1166. Works in the area of information management, promotes patient care through health information, and advocates for the profession on governmental, educational, social, and business issues that affect the management of veterinary health.

American Veterinary Medical Law Association. www.avmla.org. 1-312-233-2760. You do not have to be a lawyer to join their group or attend their meetings (held at each annual AVMA meeting).

Bellman, Geoffrey. 2001. *The Consultant's Calling: Bringing Who You Are to What You Do*, New and Revised Edition. Hoboken, NJ: Jossey-Bass, a division of Wiley

Block, Peter. 2011. *Flawless Consulting: A Guide to Getting Your Expertise Used*, Third Edition. Hoboken, NJ: Jossey-Bass/Pfeiffer.

Fred Pryor Seminars, Career Tracks. Division of Park University Enterprise, Inc. www.pryor.com. Includes human resources, personal development, business management, and client service seminars for the public and more.

Levinson, Jay Conrad, and Michael W. McLaughlin. 2004. *Guerrilla Marketing for Consultants: Breakthrough Tactics for Winning Profitable Clients*. Hoboken, NJ: John Wiley & Sons.

National Speakers Association. www.nsaspeaker.org. 1-480-968-2552.

Nickols, Fred. 2003. "The Consulting Process: A Bare Bones Outline." *Skullworks*. home.att.net/~nickols/articles.htm. www.skullworks.com. nickols@att.net.

Presentations Magazine. www.presentations.com. Focuses on how to give good presentations (speeches, seminars, etc., including computer software for making slides). It's free for qualified subscribers (you must have some kind of influence in purchasing decisions).

Society for Human Resource Management. www.shrm.org. 1-800-283-7476. Provides a wealth of information, articles, and continuing education.

Stanford University. www.smi.stanford.edu/community. 1-650-723-6979. Offers a one-week medical informatics short course.

Toastmasters. www.toastmasters.org. Helps people become better speakers; look into local groups for contact information.

University of Missouri online master's degree program in Health Informatics. www.hmi.missouri.edu. 1-800-877-4764. Prepares professionals to respond to the changing dynamics of health care by providing them with the skills necessary to develop, apply, and evaluate the use of information technology in the health-care arena. The program is designed to produce professionals who can lead organizations in the application of information technology to improve the delivery of health care. Graduates follow a variety of career paths to become chief informatics officers, systems developers, software designers, consultants, and more.

Veterinary Hospital Managers Association. www.vhma.org. 1-877-599-2707.

VetPartners. www.vetpartners.org.

Weiss, Alan. 2002. *Value-Based Fees: How to Charge and Get What You're Worth.* The Ultimate Consultant Series. Hoboken, NJ: Pfeiffer.

Computer-Related Jobs

Nanette Walker, MEd, RVT, LVT, CVT, has worked in the veterinary profession for 24 years. She currently oversees the Veterinary Support Personnel Network (VSPN), an online community for all support staff working under the direction of a licensed veterinarian. Because the veterinarians who began Veterinary Information Network (VIN) realized that they could not do their job without the veterinary support team, they created VSPN.

Nanette supervises the content of the Web site, coordinates CE courses, manages both paid and volunteer staff, and has seen much success with the company. She does what comes naturally to her, being a source of communication and networking.

Nanette advises: "You are embarking on the most incredible journey of your life. Keep an open mind, embrace change, take advantage of opportunities, and never let anyone hold you back from achieving your dream. Too often in our profession, we settle for what we think is okay. Be the instigator of positive, professional, forward motion in your life and in your workforce."

Information Services and Software

Working in information services or informatics is a combination of writing and computer work. Options include writing for database vendors and designing or writing content for software programs. Online vendors may hire technicians to answer pet owners' questions or to write columns (see Chapter 11, "Writing, Editing, and Publishing").

These fields are rather new, so there's still room for people without formal training beyond the technician degree to find jobs in informatics. Also, many positions in government combine these information skills and knowledge of medical terminology with other work.

Information services

Technicians may be hired to help write abstracts or gather database information. Although library science professionals or technical writers are often used for this purpose, there is sometimes a need for a professional with the ability to understand medical terminology and complex studies. Technicians may be hired on a full-time or part-time basis, as employees or freelancers. Titles of full-time positions vary but include *research literature analyst* and *technical information specialist*.

There are many services that provide indexes or abstracts of medical or veterinary literature. These services need someone to review, index, or write abstracts of scientific literature and to do literature searches. Other organizations, universities, and companies have ongoing needs for literature searching, abstracting, or indexing. For instance, the National Agricultural Library has a policy of hiring people with science backgrounds as technical information specialists.

Daily work

Duties and basic qualifications for many of these jobs are similar. They include a love of reading, basic computer skills (especially working with a database), and writing skills. The work involves a lot of reading and typing. Working indoors and at a desk may not appeal to some people.

Computer work is necessarily an indoor desk job, although with newer technology (wireless Internet), a laptop computer can go anywhere. The low level of contact with animals (and sometimes people) is desired by some technicians. Others manage to balance their love of computers with a need to interact with people by working in sales or technical support. These jobs provide great mental stimulation and an easy way to keep up on the latest information in veterinary medicine. Many jobs include reading journals and books and researching information on Web sites about veterinary medicine (sometimes in foreign languages).

Pay

Pay depends on the type of company or government job held. Qualified freelancers charge fees of $25 per hour and up; respected, experienced freelancers may charge hourly rates ranging from $50 to $150 per hour.

Qualifications

Although there are no standard qualifications for this type of work, you must be able to show that you have the necessary medical writing and/or computer software skills. Demonstrate this by showing previous work experience and examples of written materials. Begin a portfolio of your medical articles and presentations. Catalog your chats, input, and participation on Web sites related to veterinary medicine. Catalog your articles appearing in state professional organizations' newsletters. Keep copies of materials written for 4-H groups, for columns in local newspapers, and for pet-related publications. Ask colleagues to critique work in a professional, direct way. Find a mentor, one you respect, and learn from your mentor's experiences. Then become a mentor. Look for the opportunity for exchange between generations within the veterinary community to broaden your horizons.

Informatics training is offered at many universities. One such program is the health informatics training offered at the University of Missouri in Columbia. This degree

> prepares professionals to respond to the changing dynamics of health care, by providing them with the skills necessary to develop, apply, and evaluate the use of information technology in the health care arena. The Health Informatics (HI) master's program is designed to produce professionals who can lead organizations in the application of information technology to improve the delivery of health care. HI program graduates follow a variety of career paths to become Chief Informatics Officers (CIOs), systems developers, software designers, consultants, and many more. (www.hmi.missouri.edu/, 1-800-877-7464)

The Stanford Section on Medical Informatics offers a one-week introductory course on medical informatics, held at the Stanford campus each summer (www.smi.stanford.edu/community/, 1-650-723-6979). The course includes lectures, computer labs, and research project descriptions/demos. There are morning lectures, afternoon hands-on computer laboratory sessions, and project presentations and demonstrations of medical informatics research at Stanford.

Online courses are outlined on various Web sites, including the following:
- Course Advisor, www4.courseadvisor.com/wiz/stageonesubmit/65291908
- Stanford Biomedical Informatics, bmi.stanford.edu/
- New Horizons Computer Learning Centers, www.newhorizons.com

To find the New Horizons center nearest you, enter your zip code.

To start
Freelancers often find jobs through word of mouth (see Chapter 1, "Preparing

to Enter the Job Market"). The following methods apply to both freelance and employee jobs:

- In the federal government (see Chapter 15, "Working for the Federal Government" section), contact the Office of Personnel Management and look for jobs in "technical writing" or "information services." Potential hiring agencies might include the National Library of Medicine (National Institutes of Health [NIH]), the National Agricultural Library (U.S. Department of Agriculture [USDA]), and the National Technical Information Service (Department of Commerce), usgovinfo.about.com /bljobsusda.htm.
- Check the classified ads of newspapers.
- Chat with industry representatives at any large veterinary convention. Look for exhibits by companies that make diagnostic software or databases.
- Attend meetings of the associations listed in Chapter Resources.
- Start your own business. You could sell computer consulting services, a software product that you designed, or your services as a journal abstract writer.
- Attend the Medical Library Association's annual meeting; chat with database vendors in the exhibit hall. Librarians are technical information specialists who must know a great deal about database management. Go to www.mlanet.org or call 1-312-419-9094.

National agricultural library

As one of the most comprehensive sources of U.S. agricultural and life sciences information, the AGRICOLA (Agricultural Online Access) database contains bibliographic records for documents acquired by the National Agricultural Library (NAL) of the USDA. AGRICOLA serves as the document locator and bibliographic control system for the NAL collection, covering the field of agriculture in the broadest sense. The NAL hires technical information specialists for indexing.

NAL jobs are advertised through the USDA: usgovinfo.about.com/bljobsusda .htm. Foreign-language ability is not required, but computer skills and the ability to use online databases are necessary.

Computer software

Veterinary software includes diagnostic programs, business management programs, herd health–monitoring programs (dairy production, nutritional analysis), and database programs (journals, abstracts, or seminars on disk).

Technicians may work with computer software in two main ways: by writing programs and by performing sales or technical assistance for a software company. Companies that write computerized diagnostic programs may hire technicians to write some of the program content. Entrepreneur technicians may also write their own software programs for sale to veterinary hospitals.

As the field becomes more specialized and the amount of technical expertise grows, it is likely that many technicians doing this type of work will have had additional training in the area of computer software (by on-the-job training or by taking classes).

Online marketing specialist

Many technicians have an interest and expertise in using social networking, a part of marketing. If you are interested in pursuing social networking for your veterinary hospital, consider reading *Social Media for Veterinary Professionals*, a short, concise, and informative book by Brenda Tassava, CVPM, CVJ. Keep in mind that social media are about building relationships and connecting with your clients and the veterinary industry. If you plan to simply create a page or two on Twitter or Facebook that show your office hours and discounts, you won't really be a social media specialist. On the other hand, if you want to tell stories, post photos, and inform your clients of the stellar services your hospital provides, then this may be a career path for you.

Once you have your management's support, create goals, timelines, rules for posting, ideas for engaging the community, and definitions of success. Be realistic about the amount you can contribute per day, week, or month, and make sure you can keep up the pace for a year or longer.

Before you take your business page live, consider the emotional aspects of the relationships you are building. Social media are all about connecting to your clients on a personal level, not about sales. Those who join the circle of friends of your veterinary hospital typically want to do the following:

- Learn more about veterinary medicine and what your veterinary hospital does
- Feel connected to the team and stay in the loop
- Care for the pets they love and cherish

In your role, you must help them achieve those goals.

Sara Crisp is a veterinary technician in Portland, Oregon. She works at a 24-hour emergency clinic and has started managing her practice's Facebook and Twitter accounts.

Computerized Medical Equipment and Hardware

Hardware is the term used to refer to desktop computer equipment. Today, many pieces of equipment used in veterinary medicine are computer-based or involve computer technology, such as digital radiography and many types of lab equipment. A technician with an interest in computers could find work in a wide variety of companies, servicing or selling such products. This could involve working for the company that manufactures the equipment (see Chapter 12, "Careers in Vterinary Industry").

A wide variety of equipment is digitized/computerized with hardware that needs updates and maintenance, including laboratory equipment and diagnostic equipment (ultrasound, endoscope).

Radiographic equipment requires continued maintenance and certification. Working on this type of equipment requires state credentialing. The digital portion of the system is usually managed by the manufacturer's support personnel. There are various manufacturers for both the tables and the digital plates/cameras.

With the introduction of computer radiography (CR) and direct digital radiography (DR), a veterinary technician now has an opportunity to enter a new and growing area of diagnostic imaging not as a hardware specialist but as a liaison between the manufacturer and the hospital, a user, and a trainer. "Joining the digital imaging revolution can be a most exciting experience and may well be the wave of the future for all diagnostic imaging modalities," writes Donna Tudor, BS, RT, in the *NAVTA Journal*. Her article outlines advantages and disadvantages of both techniques. Visiting an exhibitor at a local veterinary convention may be very informative. Since this is still a relatively new concept, the booth attendants are eager to tell the veterinary community of the wonderful service CR/DR provides.

There is a society for veterinary ultrasound enthusiasts. The International Veterinary Ultrasound Society organizes an annual meeting focused on ultrasound education in research and its use in veterinary medicine. This group is sponsored and supported by the manufacturers of ultrasound machines. Continuing education classes involve both hands-on and class interpretation (viewing ultrasound pictures) sessions. The society offers a certificate program. Veterinary technicians may want to use this to advantage in large- and small-animal veterinary medicine. Visit www.ivuss.org for more information.

As Jim Nash, MHA, CVPM, hospital administrator at Community Pet Hospital in Thornton, Colorado, says, "Many technicians in practice take on other important operational responsibilities. Often these tasks require a level of expertise and involve some level of technology. Whether it be fixing lab equipment or managing digital radiographs, these skills are transferable to other careers within veterinary medicine. Many industry companies seek out credentialed technicians as their understanding of hospital operations lends a greater appreciation of customer needs."

A wide variety of other technology is used in medicine. Visit the exhibit hall of any large veterinary meeting to view new ideas, such as therapeutic point lasers or exercise treadmills.

Chapter Resources

American Association of Corporate and Public Practice Veterinarians. www.aacppv.org. 1-916-726-1560. Includes veterinarians who work for industry, which includes computer business. Join and attend one of their meetings to network and find new opportunities.

American Medical Informatics Association (AMIA). www.amia.org. 1-301-657-1291. Dedicated to the development and application of medical informatics in support of patient care, teaching, research, and health-care administration. It holds an annual conference, a computer applications symposium, and professional specialty group meetings; publishes the journals *Computers and Biomedical Research* and *MD Computing;* and offers discounts on medical informatics software.

Association for Veterinary Informatics. www.avinformatics.org. 1-425-455-0727. Promotes the use of informatics by veterinarians; its newsletter includes information about informatics short courses and fellowships (for students and graduates), as well as new software, computer resources, etc. Past newsletters can be found on the Web site.

Ellis, David. 2000. *Technology and the Future of Health Care: Preparing for the Next 30 Years.* Jossey-Bass.

Information Technology Association of America. www.itaa.org. 1-703-522-5055. A trade association for those involved with information technology. It offers newsletters, meetings, and seminars.

International Association of Business Communicators. www.iabc.com. 1-415-544-4700.

International Conferences of Animal Health Information Specialists. www.vmls.mlanet .org. Originally organized by members of the Veterinary Medical Libraries Section/ Medical Library Association to enhance the flow of animal health information worldwide. The conferences are directed to librarians and other information professionals working in veterinary medicine, laboratory animal science, and zoological and wildlife medicine. Proceedings of past conferences are available.

Medical Library Association. www.mlanet.org. 1-312-419-9094. Has a subsection for veterinary librarians and a job placement service (free for members; a fee is charged for nonmembers). The annual meeting in May has hands-on computer courses (you can buy recordings of the talks). The meeting is worth attending for its exhibit hall alone, which is full of database vendors and suppliers to talk to about abstracting jobs.

National Federation of Abstracting and Information Services. www.nfais.org. 1-215-893-1561. An organization of the world's leading publishers of databases and information services in the sciences, engineering, social sciences, business, the arts, and the humanities, representing the for-profit, nonprofit, and government sectors. Members are the international leaders in information collection, organization, and dissemination.

Roos, Dave. "Step Up Your Technology." *Veterinary Economics*, July 2006. veterinarybusiness. dvm360.com/vetec/article/articleDetail.jsp?id=357465.

Smith, Ronald D., and Mitsuko Williams. 2000. "Applications of Informatics in Veterinary Medicine." *Bulletin of the Medical Library Association*, January. www.pubmedcentral.nih.gov. Defines informatics applications within the veterinary community. Veterinary medical articles researched; free digital archives.

Society for the Internet in Medicine. www.internet-in-medicine.org. Promotes education of the public and the medical community in applications of the Internet and related technologies in the fields of medical sciences, health-care practice, and management. Members are eligible for reduced registration fees for society events, including MEDNET—The World Congress of the Internet in Medicine—and a reduction in the subscription cost to the journal *Medical Informatics*.

Society of Technical Communicators. www.stc.org. 1-703-522-4114. An organization of technical writers and a great resource.

Tudor, Donna. 2008. "Introduction to Digital Imaging." *NAVTA Journal*, Fall.

Tassava, Brenda. 2010. *Social Media for Veterinary Professionals: Online Community, Reputation, and Brand Management*. Lulu Press.

Veterinary Support Personnel Network (VSPN). www.vspn.org. 1-530-756-4881. Offers online chats, continuing education, and communication boards for the veterinary team, technicians, receptionists, assistants, and veterinarians. If you are a student or are interested in taking the Veterinary Technician National Exam (VTNE), VSPN offers test review sessions twice a year. There is a nominal cost.

VETINFO. www.vetinfo.com. An Internet mailing list for discussing veterinary medical informatics and use of computers in veterinary medicine.

Vetlib-L. www.listserv.net/scripts/wl.exe?SL1=VETLIB-L&H=LISTSERV.VT.EDU. An online discussion list for veterinary librarians and those interested in the field. Vetlib-L is a listserv for seeking articles and requests, assisting librarians with information.

Writing, Editing, and Publishing

Veterinary technicians who enjoy writing and reading may find themselves drawn to a career in the writing, editing, and publishing world. It isn't always the easiest career to get started in, but it can be very intellectually rewarding. Some of the positions are full-time but others are freelance, so be sure to refer to Chapter 5, "Starting Your Own Business."

Freelance Writing

Although very few technicians make a living as full-time writers, writing is an integral part of any career path. For many veterinary technicians, freelance writing is something they can do "on the side," with their main income coming from other work.

Having your writing published can earn you the respect of your colleagues, spread the word about your other work, or give you a creative outlet. Whether you are writing full-time or part-time, you must understand the business of writing.

One sure way to make a good living as a full-time writer is to get a job with the government. You may be hired by any one of the main government agencies, from the Fish and Wildlife Service to the National Institutes of Health, as a technical writer. For more information, see "Working for the Federal Government" in Chapter 15, or browse the list of federal job vacancies at the Office of Personnel Management's Web site at www.usajobs.opm.gov.

Writing magazine articles

Jenny Sullivan, the managing editor of John Lyons's *Perfect Horse*, has this to say about writing about veterinary medicine: "For me, writing comes with an awesome amount of responsibility. I realize that readers will make decisions based on what words I choose, so I take this very seriously. Because of my background and credentials [as a technician], I am perceived to have more credibility as a writer/editor. I also have many of my own technical resources, so I typically don't need a lot of guidance on article development." She also works as an editor and shares the following insight:

> Interestingly enough, I have many of the same challenges as an editor that I had when I was a tech. Time management is a huge issue. I'm constantly striving to meet deadlines and wrangling writers to get articles in on time. I used to do the same thing with client appointments and keeping doctors on schedule! I've also become a master multitasker. I'm editing stories for one issue, choosing photographs for another issue, and handing out writing assignments for a third issue. I used to do the same thing with X-rays on one dog, a blood draw on another, and a treatment due on a third.

She encourages technicians: "If you have writing skills and interest in the area, put yourself out there! Good writers are hard to find in the veterinary field, so make sure everyone knows about you! Network, network, network!

Technicians working in academia, or for their specialty requirements, may think of writing in terms of technical research articles for peer-reviewed scientific journals. Peer-reviewed articles differ from those written for other purposes. In academia, the writer is not paid to write; instead, the writer publishes in order to report research findings and to maintain his or her academic credentials.

In contrast, technician freelance writers are paid for their work. They write to boost their annual income or to spread the word about their other business (e.g., grooming, consulting). Technicians may write articles for a variety of magazines, journals, or newspapers. Technician-writers usually write for two major markets: technician professional journals and magazines for animal owners.

Technicians may write business or medical articles for a variety of professional journals, from *Firstline* to the *NAVTA Journal*. On a lighter note, they may write animal health-care articles for magazines like *Bird Talk*, *Western Horseman*, or *Cat Fancy*. Although the latter articles may seem simple in subject matter, writing them is not as simple as it first appears.

The full-time freelance writer is self-employed and typically has an office in the home. Freelance writers begin by coming up with an idea for an article. The writer may call or write to magazines and ask for their "writers' guidelines," which outline the style and format in which articles must be submitted. Some journals, such as *Veterinary Technician*, have a page in the monthly magazine outlining their expectations and recommendations.

The article's length, subject, and style are considered when deciding which magazine to approach. A "query letter" is written to the magazine's editor, outlining the idea. The editor then writes or calls and either turns down the idea or gives the assignment. If the article is assigned, the editor and writer discuss the payment terms and rights to be sold. A contract is sent, signed, and mailed back to the editor.

Daily work

All freelance writers use a computer and a word-processing program. The work requires self-discipline. The hardest thing about freelance writing is simply sitting down to write. Writers often set a goal of sending out two or three query letters per week. They follow up on each if they haven't heard back in about four weeks. They set up a system to keep track of all their ideas, letters sent out, and replies received, as well as assignments and their due dates.

Writing provides an uncertain income. The work is mostly done indoors, at a desk, working on a computer (which could be a pro or a con). Interaction with other people and pets is minimal. On the other hand, you control your working hours, and you can give your career a huge boost when you become published. You learn something new with every article you write, and you often get to interview interesting people in the process.

Pay

Writing articles does not pay well, partly because veterinary technician publications are accustomed to getting material for free from technicians who want to get published and who sell their material for little or nothing. Pet magazines are similarly accustomed to receiving huge volumes of material from pet-loving writers who are willing to write for low pay; for example, most major pet magazines (*Cat Fancy, Horse Illustrated, AKC Purebred Dog Gazette, Western Horseman*) pay $200 to $500 for an article.

There are a vast number of such magazines; visit a large bookstore to see some of the choices. Also, magazines that publish contributed articles are listed in *Writer's Market*, which is updated annually.

You cannot make a living writing magazine articles if you limit yourself to writing for magazines that focus on pets or animals. Although you may be able to write an article in a day or two, it is a challenge to sell an article every day. The best you can hope for is, at some point, to be hired to write a monthly column, so you get a regular but small trickle of income. Once this happens, you are listed on the magazine's masthead as a "consulting" or "contributing" editor, a feather in your cap and something to put on your resumé.

There is a bigger market for pet articles than just pet magazines. Many women's and home magazines also run articles about animals. The major women's magazines (*Good Housekeeping*, *Woman's Day*, etc.) pay well for an article ($1,000 and up), but becoming a regular contributor is extremely unlikely. There are thousands of freelance writers trying to break into these markets. There is no high-paying magazine that will look twice at your work until and unless you have published many articles in smaller publications and you have become very well-known (even for basic articles about fleas or worms). Start by writing articles for your local paper and accumulate a few "clips" (samples of your work) that you can send to pet magazines with your query letters.

The main reason to write is to help sell something else: another service you offer, or another product you sell. You can get a great deal of exposure ("free advertising") for your other products or services by writing articles on the same subject and mentioning your primary business in the author's bio (the short line or paragraph that follows the article). For instance, the bio for an article about grooming in a local newspaper could read, "Sue is the owner of Great Grooming Services."

Another reason to write articles is to make a name for yourself. Perhaps you then want to augment your income as a speaker, a consultant, or in some other way.

Qualifications

To be successful, freelancers must be good at selling their work. The beginning freelance writer has two hurdles to overcome (besides being able to write well). The first is to actually send out a query letter or sample article. The next is to get over the rejection slips and editorial changes to your work. When it comes to editing, hold fast to being technically correct and be ready to give on stylistic editorial changes.

Technician-writers don't have to be specialists to write well on a subject. Their technician experience and education make them experts in most people's eyes when it comes to writing for pet magazines. However, whether articles are directed at the lay public or the veterinary team, they must include interviews with other experts to create a readable, credible, and interesting article. It's those interviews that present the author as expert.

Writing successfully requires studying the business of writing. This is different from, and just as important as, studying how to write. Serious freelance writers should take three steps: join a local writers' group, read *Writer's Market* (book), and attend large writers' conferences (these are similar to large veterinary conferences, with seminars on the business of writing—from what the magazines are buying to understanding electronic rights).

Successful freelance writers have a good understanding of how magazines are published, what editors do, and what readers like to read. They study magazines so that they know the style, word count, and complexity of each magazine's articles. They then match each of their article ideas to the magazine where it fits best.

To start

Learn about copyright before you start. Then, use the book *Writer's Market* to find authors' guidelines for various publications. *Writer's Market* also outlines how to send in a query letter and other essentials of proposing an article to an editor. David Liss, BA, RVT, VTS (ECC), wrote an article outlining how veterinary technicians can step into the world of writing that can be found on the My Exceptional Veterinary Team Web site, titled "So You Want to Be a Writer?" It helps you take a thought, turn it into words, and try to get it published.

A brief overview of copyright for freelance writers

Freelance writers are self-employed writers who sell the right to use their work—articles or books—to magazines, book publishers, or veterinary-related companies. The first thing to know about your writing is that you own it until you agree otherwise in writing. Copyright law stipulates that a work is copyrighted as soon as it is recorded in tangible form—whether printed or on a computer disk.

Once you write something, you can sell partial or all rights to use your material. Many well-respected, professional writers who write articles for magazines will sell only "first North American printed serial rights," which means the purchaser has the right to be the first one to use the material in printed form in a serial (magazine). Once they do so, you may be able to resell the exact same material, at which time you are selling "reprint rights" or "second serial rights"—this means that the next purchaser gets the right to use the material one time, but that it has already been published elsewhere. Additional rights that can be sold include electronic, video, and foreign rights.

Doing "work for hire" means that you are selling all rights to your material to the person who hires you. If you agree to this, then, after the article is published, you do not have the right to use it in exactly the same way again, since you no longer own it. However, you can use the ideas in another form or write a similar article with a different twist.

People who write as part of their jobs as salaried employees produce work for hire. Freelancers may also agree to do work for hire. Except for technical writing (see discussion below), this may or may not be a good idea, depending on the amount of income you intend to generate exclusively from writing and whether you expect to use the article again. Once you sell all rights to a work, someone else gets all the income from any future sales of that work. Magazines can reuse your work in several ways. They can combine it with other articles on the same subject and create a book, they can reprint the same article in several magazines, and they can sell the article online to computer users. If you sell all rights, you don't receive any of the income generated for those sales. However, you can still express your ideas in another way, and you can sell the new article to a different publication. Writers should look at ways they can spin the same core idea in many different ways for various audiences. Consider the different ways you would discuss pet obesity if you were writing for veterinarians, children, pet owners, etc. Each article would be different from the others, but the core idea (how to help overweight pets) and general background research (supplemented by applicable interviews conducted for each audience) would be shared.

Many magazines present authors with a work-for-hire contract unless the author insists on different terms. It is possible for writers to change the contracts they receive for writing an article or book. Although most publishers use the same contract template for every writer, almost all contracts are to some degree negotiable. For example, you can try to negotiate for extra payment for every different form in which your work is published—including electronic form.

Many first-time writers worry that someone will "steal" their ideas for articles or books. Although this may occur, it is rare. The difficult thing to accept is that none of your ideas are original. Chances are that someone, somewhere, has thought of the same idea. So, when you send out a query letter, your goal is to convince the recipient that you are better qualified to write the piece than anyone else, and that you have a unique perspective that will make the article fresh and original. If you've done a good job of that, there is no reason for the recipient to "steal" the idea and have someone else write about it.

Writing for web sites, electronic mailing lists, or online servers

Writing content for online use is just another type of freelance writing. As part of a Web site or online provider's services, technicians may answer questions posed by other online users (usually pet owners). It is important to define the number of questions that must be answered each week and the time frame in which questions must be answered. Technicians may also write regular columns, just as they would for a print magazine, or they may write informational articles that are made available for an indefinite time to pet owners searching for specific information online.

Almost all the above information about freelancing will apply to writing Web site content. Pay for writing used online tends to be low, and many contracts stipulate that the writing be done as work for hire.

See Chapter 10, "Computer-Related Jobs," for a description of an online marketing specialist who works with social networking Web sites. This position requires writing skills as well as marketing and computer expertise.

Technical Writing

Another opportunity for freelance writing is technical writing for industry (pharmaceutical companies, pet food companies, etc.). In contrast to freelance magazine writing, it may be possible for technicians to make a living this way. Examples of technical writing include proceedings for a continuing education seminar; a booklet or brochure about a product, for use by sales staff; promotional materials for a new product; a paper for submission to a refereed, peer-reviewed journal, based on raw data from a scientific study; and educational materials for use by a company's sales team.

Daily work

The day-to-day work of a technical writer is similar to that of a writer of magazine articles: sitting at the computer in a home office, researching Web sites, reading, documenting, and typing away. Instead of sending query letters outlining an article idea, you respond to a company that asks you to do a specific project. A computer, Internet access, and a copy/fax machine are essential in this business, as well as access to overnight delivery services such as Federal Express and United Parcel Service.

Technical writers rarely get public recognition for their work. They don't expect to see their name on a refereed article they helped write, since the authors of the study (the people who performed the study about which they are writing) will be the only ones listed (the writer may get a footnote of thanks).

Technical writers must have a good understanding of the goals of the company for which they write. If they are writing a piece for publication in a refereed journal, for example, they must be able to match the material with the most appropriate journal. They then write the article so it fits the journal's requirements. At other times they may write material for a sales booklet or brochure that must be understood by its target audience.

Writing allows you to interview many interesting people who are experts in their field. You get to study and write about an incredible variety of fascinating subjects, some of which you'd never explore otherwise.

In contrast to other types of freelance writing, technical writing is usually done as "work for hire." This is not a problem, since the source of your information is usually the company itself, and the only interested user is that company. Technical writers may be asked to sign a confidentiality agreement that stipulates they will not reveal company internal information for a specified number of years. The pay is high enough to justify the work-for-hire agreement.

For information about writing for computer abstracting or database services, see Chapter 10, "Computer-Related Jobs."

Pay

Technical writing is far more lucrative than writing magazine articles. It is customary to charge by the hour (from $25 to more than $100 per hour, depending on your qualifications and the difficulty of the work) plus expenses (long-distance telephone, computer research online charges, etc.). It takes a long time to get established clients, so be ready for some lean years and keep another job on the side.

Qualifications

Excellent writing, grammar, and spelling skills are essential. Time management is also critical, since your clients expect you to deliver on time. Networking skills are important, too. Although you work mostly alone, you still must go out and meet people, networking to get continual work.

To start

Many large companies employ technical writers, but others hire freelancers for some or all jobs. One way to break in is to first call the company and ask if they hire freelancers, and if so, who decides when they are hired. Then write a letter directly to that person, including your resumé and any clips of your work. Do not expect to be called immediately; however, your letter will be filed and you may be surprised with a call months or even a year or more later, especially if you've been contacting them a few times a year to ask if they have any work for you.

The best way to get work is by networking. Get to know people who work in the industry and follow the other networking tips listed in the Introduction and Chapter 12, "Careers in Veterinary 'Industry.'" There are also full-time government and industry jobs in technical writing.

Writing a Book

Many veterinary technicians have great book ideas. If you want to write a book, you must first answer this: Do you want to make money with this book (i.e., write something that sells)? Or do you just want to produce a book for the joy of writing and providing information to those who need it? Are you willing to spend money to do so?

The answers to these questions will change your approach to writing your book. If you are interested in writing a book that will sell, you need to study the business of book writing and selling. Start by reading the books listed at the end of this section, by joining your local writers' group, and by reading writers' magazines (see discussion above).

It is rare for a writer to start a career by writing a book. Few publishers will consider an idea presented by someone who has never published an article in a magazine. So, if you jumped to this section and skipped the section "Writing Magazine Articles," go back and read it.

Many book authors have an agent. An agent represents the author, presenting the book proposal to a variety of publishers until it is sold. The agent then helps the author negotiate the book contract. Some agents continue to assist the author after a book is published, helping with marketing ideas and sale of subsidiary rights (e.g., book excerpts sold to magazines, foreign rights). Use of an agent is optional and depends on the amount of energy authors want to put into selling and marketing their books. Fiction works have a greater need for an agent's expertise than do nonfiction ones. (A publisher can more easily make a quick decision about a nonfiction book based on a book proposal alone because the book subject and scope are readily apparent.)

Another option, self-publishing a book, should be undertaken only when the book's intended audience is small or occupies a narrow niche. Authors who self-publish a book because no publisher will buy it often find that no one else will buy it, either. Successful self-publishing is done by experienced authors who have the time and knowledge to attend to all aspects of book production and marketing.

Because writing a book is rarely a career in itself, we won't go into book writing in detail. Once you enter the world of writing, attend writers' seminars, and read more about writing, the business of writing a book will become much clearer.

Magazine or Journal Editing

Colorado Association of Certified Veterinary Technicians member Jenny Merchant, CVT, has edited the association's newsletter for six years. She has generously given her talents for the betterment of her profession. She is also a freelance writer for the American Animal Hospital Association. She works at a referral center and in her spare time researches papers, edits newsletters, and adds income to her technician wages.

An editor is responsible for the content of the publication. There are a limited number of paid jobs available in editing veterinary publications. This may be a great venue for volunteering, especially for the not-for-profit organizations that generate newsletters for their members.

Daily work

Editing includes reading manuscripts that are submitted for publication; critiquing these and consulting with authors about changes and improvements (changes in style, sentence structure, scientific content, etc.); deciding which articles to include in each issue, and how the issue should be organized; deciding what types of columns or regular features to publish; reading letters to the editor and deciding which to print; and doing some writing of your own, too. That translates to lots of time sorting through and reading mail; talking on the telephone; writing letters (to authors, explaining rejections and revisions); and marking up articles as they are read with questions, comments, and corrections for the author.

Editors spend most of their time at a desk, but their jobs are very much "people" jobs. Most editor jobs require that the staff live in the community where the magazine is produced (usually a city).

The editor has to enjoy working with and supervising people, giving helpful corrections, and, of course, must love reading, writing, and words. The drawbacks include working with difficult authors, losing time reading unusable material, and struggling to meet deadlines. Magazines that rely on advertising income have a delicate balancing act, in that there may be pressure not to print material that denigrates a big advertiser.

Other kinds of editing work are copyediting for sense, organization, consistency, fact checking, grammar, punctuation, and spelling; this work is usually done by a nonveterinary person, but someone with a strong background in writing and editing and eagerness to take continuing education courses can try this field as well. Technical editing is often assigned to specialists (for technical comments and suggestions for revision). Copyeditors and technical editors (reviewers) work with the magazine's editors, who have final say in whether or not an article is published. Consulting editors, contributing editors, and editorial advisers are usually freelancers, not staff (see "Freelance Writing" above).

Pay

According to Salary.com, full-time magazine editorial jobs pay between $45,000 and $65,000 per year, depending on qualifications. (Most editors have a bachelor's or master's degree.) However, you should expect lower pay for part-time work such as editing newsletters for smaller associations. Some associations may pay the editor by the job (per newsletter) or by the hour, or they may depend on volunteers.

Qualifications

Qualifications for editorial jobs include good writing skills, writing experience, love of words and reading, and an ability to interpret and analyze scientific studies for accuracy and logic. Having an interest in working with people is essential, as is the ability to give authors tactful, constructive criticism and advice in a positive and helpful manner. Article authors sometimes have strong egos—especially when they are experts in their field—and can be difficult to work with. Editors must be comfortable with computer word processing and electronic mail. Editors of scientific and technical publications may need a background in research or knowledge of statistics.

To start

Job possibilities include editor-in-chief, associate editor, and assistant editor. The editor-in-chief of a magazine is generally someone who has worked as an assistant or associate editor at the same or another, similar magazine. Your best approach may be to apply for a job as an assistant editor.

For information about potential openings with any veterinary publication, write to the publisher or editor-in-chief listed on the magazine's masthead. Be sure to write to the address listed for editorial offices (not the address for subscriptions or advertising). Take a look at the mastheads of veterinary and pet journals to see which ones have veterinary technicians on staff.

Multimedia

Multimedia is a term that refers to the use of print materials, video, computers, and television to convey information. Many veterinary-related companies create their own multimedia materials (see Chapter 12, "Careers in Veterinary 'Industry'"). Others hire an outside firm to do this work.

Multimedia companies utilize photographers, computer software designers, graphic designers, and writers. Writers create scripts or content for multimedia.

Veterinary Learning Systems (VLS) is an example of a company that works to serve the multimedia needs of the veterinary profession. VLS assists companies with marketing their products to veterinarians and their teams. They create videotapes, books, CDs, scripts, and other materials. VLS also produces two journals, organizes meetings for companies, and assists companies with their customer service needs.

VLS employees perform a wide variety of tasks, from arranging space for meetings to editing technical material. Their jobs involve negotiating, working with people, and travel. They understand and are comfortable with marketing, enjoy writing and words, and spend much of their time on the telephone and answering mail. They constantly learn about new products and medications. More than half of their time is spent working at a desk (www.vetlearn.com).

A rapidly growing niche for veterinary technicians may be the creation of hospital-generated continuing education using multimedia. As a teaching hospital, 24-hour veterinary hospital DoveLewis (www.dovelewis.org) also focuses on educating interns and veterinary and technician students. They collaborate with both Oregon and Washington State Universities and the nearby veterinary technician programs. The team members are passionate about educating, and it shows. Head technician Megan Brashear, CVT, VTS (ECC), oversees the technician-related continuing education and has this to say about her career: "My favorite part of DoveLewis is teaching and training. We wouldn't be able to save as many lives as we do if not for the ability of our staff to mentor and train each other. I want to inspire them to always want more for themselves and for their patients. The opportunity to mentor technicians and reach out to the community are some of the most rewarding parts of my job."

The veterinary technicians at DoveLewis are empowered and entrusted to create their continuing education videos: a technician does all the camera shots, editing, and producing; Megan oversees the creation of the programs; and an assistant is charge of posting them on Facebook and Twitter.

Television and Radio

Although technicians do appear on television and radio programs, few are able to make this a full-time job with a focus on veterinary medicine.

Technicians who work with the news media typically do so for various reasons: to promote their other work (a book or their veterinary hospital), for the fun of it, to improve their speaking skills, to improve their image to the public or their clients, or to help educate the public.

Thomas F. Dock, BS, CVJ, is a Certified Veterinary Journalist working for Veterinary News Network. He offers this advice about seeking a career in media:

"The advantage to being a certified veterinary journalist is that news media producers, editors, and news directors will see you as a true expert. The credential will help separate the experts (veterinarians and veterinary technicians) from lay people, breeders, or trainers. …Technicians can make a huge difference in how thousands to millions of people care for their pets through their media work, not just writing, but also through on-camera work, radio interviews, …podcasts, blogs, and social media."

Because of the celebrity persona of television and radio, technicians who make such appearances are viewed by some of the public as exceptionally qualified. After all, if they weren't, why would the program interview them? This perception is only partially correct. The reality is that knowing the right people, making the right contacts, and being able to speak clearly, with animation and in sound bites, are important factors in getting on television or radio programs. For television, a good visual impression is important: professional attire, good grooming, and quiet body language (no fidgeting).

Let's say you are a consultant or a writer, and you want to make some media appearances to help sell your book or consulting services. Or perhaps you are an owner of a pet store and think you can get new customers by appearing on the local news. It will be easier for you to get on a radio show because there are so many more radio than television stations.

The first question to ask yourself is this: What programs are your potential customers watching or listening to? Unless you have written a pet-care book that is directed at the general public, there's no point in appearing on the *Today Show*. (Besides, they won't give you a second look unless your book is selling exceptionally well or is really different.)

Start by either searching the Web or going to the library and looking up the names and addresses of local or specialty television and radio shows. Specialty shows include television and radio segments devoted to pets or livestock. Send them a press release announcing your news (you must have something newsworthy to say or there's no reason to have you appear). An example might be an announcement about your new pet-sitting service or your free classes on bird care at the local senior citizens' center. Another announcement might be that your new book, *101 Training Tips for Your Cat*, just received an award, and you and your trained cat will be hosting a book signing at the local bookstore.

Follow up your press release with a phone call. If you're scheduled for an appearance, ask what you will be expected to discuss and how long the interview will last. You can even volunteer to send a list of typical questions they might ask (this is routine and makes their work easier). During the show, remember that it will be impossible for you to say everything you want to say, so don't try. Make sure the station receptionist has your contact information (listeners who want to contact you will call the station; the person who answers the phone should have your name, email address, and phone number handy). Video- or tape-record all your appearances or radio interviews and watch or listen to them to learn from your mistakes.

Chapter Resources

See also resources in Chapter 9, "Consulting," and Chapter 10, "Computer-Related Jobs."

Crawford, Tad. 2005. *Business & Legal Forms for Authors and Self-Publishers.* New York: Allworth Press.

Gould, Jay R., and Wayne A. Losano. 2008. *Opportunities in Technical Writing.* Columbus, OH: McGraw-Hill.

Hammerich, Irene, and Claire Harrions. 2001. *Developing Online Content: The Principles of Writing and Editing for the Web.* Hoboken, NJ: Robert Ipsen.

Liss, David, BA, RVT, VTS (ECC). 2012. "So You Want to Be a Writer?" *Exceptional Veterinary Team*, September. www.myevt.com/columns/95/so-you-want-be-writer.

Local writers' associations. Consider joining a local writers' group, even if you belong to a national association. Look for a group that focuses on the business of writing nonfiction (rather than just reading and critiquing one another's work). Watch your newspaper's community calendar for a listing of a writers' group. If you don't find one, ask at your library or call the newspaper.

National Writers Union. www.nwu.org. 1-212-254-0279. Web site provides analysis of electronic media and the future of copyright, and responds to concerns about access to information.

Scott, Gini Graham. 2007. *Sell Your Book, Script, or Column: How to Write a Winning Query and Make a Winning Pitch.* ASJA Press.

U.S. Copyright Office. www.copyright.gov. 1-202-702-3000. Answers general questions about copyright.

Writers' seminars. Consider attending a writers' seminar just as you attend veterinary continuing education meetings. Note seminars listed in *Writer's Digest* magazine.

The Writer. www.writermag.com. 1-800-533-6644.

Writer's Digest. www.writersdigest.com. Contact via e-mail at www.writersdigest.com/ContactUs.

Writer's Market. Published annually by Writer's Digest Books. It contains names and addresses of book publishers and agents as well as information on how to write a query letter, all about copyright, how to target your market, and all the basics of the business of writing. It lists hundreds of magazines (their pay scale, types of articles they accept, and name and address of the editor to write to). Available in any large bookstore.

Editing

American Agricultural Editors Association. www.ageditors.com. 1-952-758-6502.

Association of American Publishers. www.publishers.org. 1-202-347-3375. Conducts a course in publishing scholarly journals, among others.

Council of Science Editors (CSE; formerly the Council of Biology Editors). www.councilscienceeditors.org. 1-703-437-4377. Established in 1957 by joint action of the National Science Foundation and the American Institute of Biological Sciences. Its purpose is to improve communication in the life sciences by educating authors, editors, and publishers; to provide means of cooperation among persons interested in publishing in the life sciences; and to promote effective communication practices in primary and secondary publishing in any form. Any individual interested in the purpose of the CSE is eligible for regular membership.

Patterson, B. R., and C. E. P. Patterson. 2003. *The Editor-In-Chief: A Practical Management Guide for Magazine Editors.* Iowa State University Press.

Folio. www.foliomag.com. The magazine for magazine management; sign up for email announcements.

Freelance Writing

American Society of Journalists and Authors (ASJA). www.asja.org. 1-212-997-0947 (voice mail). A national organization of independent nonfiction writers who have met the society's standards of professional achievement. The Web site provides valuable free information to freelance writers, including contract tips, current facts and fictions about electronic publishing, and a chronology of *ASJA Contracts Watch*, an excellent source of news and information about publishers' contracts and concessions on electronic rights.

American Society of Veterinary Journalists. www.asvj.org. Offers a certification process to become a Certified Veterinary Journalist.

Cat Writer's Association. www.catwriters.org. Has many veterinarian and technician members. Newsletter and annual meeting with educational seminars. Its newsletter, *MEOW*, is issued quarterly for members only.

Dog Writer's Association of America. www.dwaa.org. Established in 1935, it has many veterinarian and technician members. It has a newsletter and an annual meeting. Contact the officers for direct inquiries, www.dwaa.org/officers.htm.

Harper, Timothy, ed. 2003. *ASJA Guide to Freelance Writing: A Professional Guide to the Business, for Nonfiction Writers of All Experience Levels.* New York: St. Martin's Griffin.

North American Agricultural Journalists. www.naaj.net.

Veterinary News Network. www.myvnn.com.

Technical Writing

Alred, Gerald J. 2005. *Handbook of Technical Writing*, Eighth Edition. New York: Bedford/St. Martin's.

American Association of Corporate and Public Practice Veterinarians (formerly the Association of Industrial Veterinarians). www.aacppv.org. 1-916-726-1560. Offers great networking opportunities at its lunch meetings, held during major veterinary conferences. Join to get to know people in industry.

American Medical Writer's Association. www.amwa.org. 1-301-294-5303. Produces a monthly "job market sheet" with lists of freelance, part-time, and full-time jobs for medical writers and editors.

Anderson, Paul V. 2006. *Technical Communication: A Reader-Centered Approach*, Sixth Edition. Independence, KY: Wadsworth Publishing.

Society for Technical Communication. www.stc.org. 1-703-522-4114. Exists to "engage in scientific, literary, and educational activities designed to advance the theory and practice of the arts and sciences of technical communication through the development of better educated personnel in the field of technical communication." Its 20,000 members include technical writers, editors, graphic designers, videographers, multimedia artists, and others whose work involves making technical information available to those who need it.

Van Laan, Krista, and Catherine Julian. 2001. *The Complete Idiot's Guide to Technical Writing*. Alpha Books.

Writing a Book

Larsen, Michael. 2004. *How to Write a Book Proposal*, Third Edition. Blue Ash, OH: Writer's Digest Books.

Poynter, Dan. 2006. *The Self-Publishing Manual: How to Write, Print, and Sell Your Own Book*, Fifteenth Edition. Santa Barbara, CA: Para Publishing.

Careers in Veterinary "Industry": Companies that Serve the Veterinary Profession

Sherrie Brosig, CVT, has worked in veterinary hospitals and has managed and been a leader in her state professional association. She is currently working for a corporation and is in the process of starting her own consulting business. She has this to say about her current career as a technician working as a territory manager for an animal health supply corporation: "Be aggressive. You will not get the money you are worth or get to do the things that you are capable of doing if you do not get in there and get it done. Don't spend life as a bystander. Also, I would say that you generally do not make the money that you are worth but the money that you negotiate for. Show how valuable you are because you are invaluable!"

When asked about the most challenging part of her career, Sherrie responded, "The time consumption. Most people think that sales representatives don't work very hard, but the good ones work all the time. I work from 5 a.m. when I get up until 11 p.m. when I go to bed."

Veterinary Industry

Technician students often hear the words *veterinary industry* and get a negative picture of a pushy sales representative. That unfortunate stereotype could not be more wrong. Let's start by getting rid of the word *industry* and instead look at specific jobs serving the veterinary profession and its large community.

A wide variety of companies make products or perform services for veterinarians and pet owners, including medications, medical supplies, medical equipment, pet foods, laboratory supplies, equipment, and insurance (for businesses, pets, and livestock). Technicians are employed in every business that manufactures, provides, or distributes these products and services. These technicians may hold an associate's of applied science or higher degree.

When you are passionate about your job, everyone you speak with is a networking opportunity. Always make a good first impression and always be prepared to learn.

Daily work

Some jobs in these companies allow you to continue to work with animals or with pet and livestock owners; others allow you to interact with other technicians, veterinarians, and the veterinarian team. All require that you use the knowledge you gained in technician school, even if it does not involve hands-on animal work. Job duties range from technical support (providing information about the company's products to veterinary teams) to management to clinical research. Many of these jobs require extensive travel. Positions are available in several departments or areas. Typical departments that employ technicians include the following:

- Marketing
- Product registration
- Production
- Quality control
- Regulatory affairs
- Research and development
- Sales
- Technical service

To earn promotions and advance your career, you should, over time, take positions in more than one department, and you should be willing to move between companies or to other parts of the country. Often, a higher salary or promotion means advancing into a management position, which takes you away from working with animals, animal owners, or veterinary teams. Many technicians elect not to pursue promotions because they prefer to live in one place and are happy with their jobs. Technicians must think outside the box if they wish to propose telecommuting or other arrangements to their employer.

Every company will have slightly different job descriptions, duties, and titles. One job in company A may have an entirely different title in company B and be divided into two jobs in company C. The descriptions that follow are offered to give you a peek at the potential choices.

Working for any veterinary-related company will invariably mean that you must already live in, or be able to move to, the city where your services are needed.

That's not always the company's headquarters, especially for technical services or sales representative jobs.

No matter what your specific job is, you represent the company for which you work, so you should have a positive opinion of its products, services, and business goals. Many jobs allow you to continue to work with animals and/or to have contact with veterinary hospitals. Pay and benefits are excellent, and there is plenty of opportunity for advancement; as with government jobs, the more you are willing to move, the faster you will advance. Many industry jobs involve a lot of travel.

All corporate employees are evaluated periodically against measurable performance criteria. For instance, you may be required to write a list of goals each year, and your raises, bonuses, and promotions are based on whether you achieve your goals. Since there is always more than enough to do, you must learn to focus on the important tasks.

Pay

Pay is generally good, with excellent benefits. Technicians working in industry consistently earn higher salaries than technicians in any other category of technician employment. Specialty technicians or those with additional degrees also see the most financial benefit from their training if they work for industry. Salaries tend to be higher in companies that produce pharmaceuticals and health products. Salaries are also higher for management positions. Most jobs in industry provide exceptional benefits, which add a significant sum to the total compensation (Bureau of Labor statistics, www.bls.gov).

Qualifications

All of these jobs require an ability to work within the structure of a business organization, including following all the company policies and procedures. You should enjoy working as part of a team and be interested in keeping up your knowledge of company products and the associated diseases or management problems. Basic computer skills and good writing and speaking skills are necessary. Experience with a wide variety of animal species and a background in statistics are helpful. Knowing how to interact with the media is useful. Companies often send their employees to speaker training or media training workshops.

Some jobs require a few years of experience in practice, whereas others require sales, managerial, or research experience. If a position looks good to you but you lack the experience, take a lower-level job and gain the experience you need for the job you really want. Good communication skills (including telephone, interpersonal, and public speaking) and writing ability will increase the inexperienced person's chances of being hired.

One thing that the veterinary industry is not looking for is a technician who just wants to get out of private practice. What company would hire someone because he or she wants to get away from something else? Instead, they're looking for people who want to get into the business—those who have a positive reason to change. They want people who may still like private practice but are looking for a greater challenge.

Searching recruiting Web sites recently revealed a wide variety of advertisements for positions in industry that require associate's or bachelor's degrees. To give you a better idea of where you're headed, here are excerpts from some of those ads. Remember that you can get the required experience by taking a lower-level job in the industry and working your way up.

Sample Job Announcements

- **Professional Services Technician:** Product support on pharmaceuticals, biologicals, other animal health products.
- **Technical Services Representative:** Must be able to work independently and make appropriate decisions with accuracy, timeliness, and complete follow-through.
- **Technical Services Veterinary Technician:** Nutritional consults, communications will provide support for all company products.
- **Territory Sales Manager:** Will be responsible for a broad geographic area with a diverse customer base to achieve sales targets.
- **Manager, Veterinary Marketing Communications:** Will build and leverage company's leadership and brand.

To start

Tip from an insider: jobs in industry are filled through a network. Who you know is as important as what you know. This needn't be a roadblock; just because you don't know anyone today doesn't mean you can't meet people starting tomorrow. Go to any large veterinary meeting and chat with the people working in the exhibit area (when they're not busy with customers). How do they like their jobs? What other jobs are available in their company? Where do they live and how much do they travel? Tell everyone you know that you are investigating jobs in industry.

If you currently have a job in private practice, chat with all the sales representatives who come in. Say yes to invitations to go out for lunch. Offer to do clinical research in your hospital for the company.

The person who has the most influence on hiring is not necessarily the person in the human resources or personnel department. Consider researching within the company to determine who it is you need to speak with regarding a job and being hired.

Focus on companies you consider to be reputable and strong, that carry quality products, and whose employees you would like as colleagues. Find out as much as you can about the company before you make your approach. Read their brochures, annual report, and any other information you can find in your local library's reference section or on the Internet.

Peruse veterinary journals for advertisements. You can also find jobs through the American Veterinary Medical Association placement service, National Association of Veterinary Technicians in America career site, and other sites (see Chapter 1, "Preparing to Enter the Job Market"). Follow up on your networking and your applications with a letter or email. Call or write after you send out your resumé, and call again every three to five months to remind them of your interest. Often personnel recruiters call people in industry, looking for someone to fill a position. If you have been persistent, your name will be remembered and passed along.

One of the biggest differences between people who have the career of their dreams and the salary that meets their needs compared with people who are in a rut and in debt is persistence!

Don't turn down a job just because it's not the exact one you want. Once you have industry experience, your choices are much greater. Why not work for a year or two as a technical services rep, for example, if it gives you an advantage when you want to apply for a job in research and development?

Insider tips on getting a job in industry

A method that is not likely to work when used by itself is to send a resumé and cover letter to the personnel or human resources department of each company you're interested in. Sending a letter to the technical services director may yield better results.

Don't go to a headhunter (recruiting) firm yourself to look for a job; headhunters look for people who aren't desperate, but who are happily working somewhere. If you call them, you appear desperate. Networking is what makes you visible to the headhunter.

The "kiss of death" is to say you hate your current job. If you hate practice, you will hate working in industry. Employers in industry want people who like practice but are looking for new challenges.

Jobs in industry are often filled through networking. Who you know is important! "Step out" and attend a convention social. You may be surprised; a company seeking a veterinary technician may have someone in the crowd looking for an outgoing, interesting, intelligent veterinary technician. You may make a valuable first impression while attending something as simple as a social.

Technical/professional service

As Julianne Galvin Evenhus, CVT, veterinary field educator, Veterinary Pet Insurance says, "As a veterinary field educator, I have the opportunity to meet with many vet tech students and discuss their expectations of their chosen profession. There seems to be a heightened concern that average salaries of technicians are not increasing to reflect their skills. Yet there are many ways to build upon your initial education to make yourself more marketable and in-demand to the veterinary world. Your career does not have to stop within the veterinary hospital walls. Technicians can choose to move on to the corporate sector as field educators, claims examiners, pharmaceutical reps, or consultants, and work for companies like Pfizer, Merck, Iams, . . . the sky's the limit!" Technical services are a good place for a technician to start a career in industry. From here, you can advance to other jobs.

A technical service representative (TSR), regional technical manager, veterinary service representative, or professional services manager learns the technical details about a company's products and uses that knowledge to answer customer questions or to train salespeople for the company. TSRs give seminars for sales staff and for practicing veterinarians and veterinary teams. They talk about their company's products or services, usually speaking in a broader sense about the disease, disorder, or injury that creates a need for that product or service—for example, a pet food company. TSRs will give talks about nutrition in relation to health and disease. The TSR may accompany sales representatives on their daily rounds to veterinary clinics, helping them answer questions and teaching them about the veterinarian-customer's concerns. They also represent the company at schools, colleges, and veterinary meetings.

TSRs may spend 50 percent or more of their time traveling; a company car is sometimes provided. Many give more than 50 lectures per year. The company may provide a PowerPoint presentation and information to be given in a talk, but the TSRs often rearrange the material to suit their needs and personal style. TSRs must become experts in the medical, insurance, nutrition, equipment, or surgical area in which their company's products or services are used. They may be in charge of handling complaints about a product, including follow-up. Time is also spent writing reports, scheduling appointments, downloading pertinent information directly to the company's server, and speaking on the phone with clients or customers.

Qualifications include willingness to travel and interest in, and preferably experience with, sales, marketing, and customer relations. Technicians who have been in private practice usually have this experience. The ability to write and speak well is a basic requirement, as is computer literacy. Being comfortable using computers is a must, but extensive knowledge is not generally required. Knowledge of Excel and PowerPoint is very useful.

Answering telephones (as a telephone consultant) can be a big part of technical services. Technicians are assigned to telephone duty to screen calls, so that the veterinarians handle only the calls that require their expertise. The technician provides information to pet owners, veterinarians, journalists, breeders, and universities about the company's products or services and may mail printed information after a telephone conversation.

The telephone consultant may interact with company workers in research and development, marketing, or the packaging/labeling department to help answer callers' questions. In some companies, technicians may be assigned to do only phone duty. Other companies have their regular TSR staff rotate—one week on phone duty, then several weeks traveling.

A technical affairs manager is responsible for a budget, strategic planning, and supervising other people. The job involves less travel than does the TSR position.

The director of professional services is in charge of the technical services department. These titles may differ within the structure of the organization, reflecting each person's talents and skills.

Research and development (R&D)

Cherylann Gieseke, BA, CVT, LATG, works for the Institutional Animal Care and Use Committee. Of her work in research and development, she says

> I have found my career in research to be challenging and rewarding. I feel that I contribute both to the well-being of animals and humans. My skills are valued and I feel that they are fully utilized. I enjoy a great deal of independence and responsibility. Working for Mayo has granted me great compensation and

benefits. Using my knowledge as a veterinary technician allows me to help investigators create their proposals. I know that the information that I provide to them will ensure that the research projects are conducted in the best possible way to minimize any pain and distress for the research animals.

On the other hand, she's found that, "because of the massive amount of regulatory control in research, there is all sorts of paperwork that must be completed. Sometimes the record-keeping and reporting requirements can seem a bit overwhelming." But ultimately, she says, "A career in veterinary technology is always interesting. You will be faced with emotional highs and lows and have days when you feel like you really made a difference and other days where no matter what you did, the outcome isn't what you wanted. Hang in there because no two days are alike, and as a veterinary technician, you do make a difference in the care of the animals in your charge."

Research and development (R&D) is the area to explore if you still want hands-on work with animals and have an interest in clinical medicine. Many positions are open to technicians, although some require additional training. Some R&D jobs allow you to stay in one place, but others require travel. Compared with other industry jobs, the hours of some R&D jobs can be long, since there are often deadlines to meet. Technicians in these jobs must be comfortable with the company's use of animals in research.

Basic research often requires specialists such as veterinary pathologists, toxicologists, and laboratory animal technicians. However, technicians may be employed as assistants to these specialists.

The R&D technician may manage the animal facility, including care and feeding of a large number of animals, treatment of sick or injured animals, and preventive health care. Technicians and veterinarians work together closely in this environment, monitoring the use of animals in research projects to ensure that experiments are both necessary and appropriate and making sure the facility passes inspection by meeting federal requirements. In most cases, the technician has advanced training in laboratory animal medicine. You may also find a position in the pet food industry, maintaining a variety of animals and assisting with preventive health care, rigorous dietary studies, food studies, and wellness programs.

For those interested in laboratory animal medicine, see Chapter 4, "Species Variety." Also look into the Academy of Surgical Research (ASR) at www.surgicalresearch.org/ (click on "Certification"), 1-952-253-6240. Veterinary technicians in research go through the ASR program, since they may perform many surgical procedures. The Academy of Surgical Research now has three levels in its certification program. The surgical research specialist certification is based upon the demonstration of ability to perform basic aseptic survival surgery on animals. The surgical research anesthetist certification is for the technician working as an anesthetist who also has responsibilities as part of the surgical team, including aseptic preparation and perioperative care for surgical patients. The surgical research technician certification is oriented toward the surgeon who performs minor surgical procedures.

Regulatory affairs and product development

Regulatory affairs jobs involve mostly desk work (writing, computer, telephone). People working in this area must interact with and be knowledgeable about the Food and Drug Administration or other applicable agency, whose regulations must be met by the company. These technicians must keep up on government regulations and new products similar to the ones they are bringing to the market. As with R&D, meeting strict deadlines may necessitate long working hours. One must have the patience to understand and deal with government regulations. Knowledge of laws, medicine, R&D, and the needs of practicing veterinarians and technicians is important. One route to jobs in regulatory affairs is experience in R&D, but a variety of backgrounds also would be appropriate for these positions, since the work differs with every project.

Sales, marketing, and education

Sales jobs involve traveling to potential buyers (veterinary clinics) to present product information and to take orders. This work may include advertising and promotion. Additional marketing may be needed to present a company's product to the veterinary profession as a whole. As competition grows among companies, the need to educate the veterinary team increases, offering more and more opportunities for motivated veterinary technicians. Some corporations hire technicians as educators to the veterinary community, yet another facet of working in industry. For example, an hourlong presentation may be given to a group of veterinarians, educating them about a disease for which your company makes a treatment.

Good news: veterinarians can fill these positions, but most sales and marketing representatives are technicians! These jobs are suited to techs who are interested in organizational tasks, working with people, and traveling. They do not involve clinical medicine but do require interacting with practicing veterinarians and veterinary teams. Jobs in marketing may require experience or additional education in that field.

Business development

Business development workers look for potential new products, negotiate deals with other companies for cooperative ventures or buyouts, and perform other business services. Usually they have business degrees, but a technical background is also necessary.

International assignments

Companies with offices overseas may have openings for technicians. Qualifications for these positions include experience in a multinational company; an understanding of the international differences in animal health markets, product development requirements, and scientific approaches; and exposure to colleagues in other countries. Fluency in a foreign language is often not required, but it is an asset and broadens your choices.

How will you get the necessary experience? Get a job in the United States working for a company that has offices in other countries so that you know its goals and methods of operation or take a temporary position with an international assistance group (see Chapter 14, "International, Volunteer, and Service Work").

Veterinary forensics

Crime Scene Investigation, veterinary style. When animal cruelty cases are investigated, veterinary technicians play a vital role in identifying the abuse, collecting evidence, and record-keeping. As Melinda Merck (2007a) writes, "The veterinary technician plays a vital role in the recognition and response to animal cruelty. They are more likely to be the first to notice signs of abuse and detect or hear something suspicious from the people who brought the animal in. Most mistakes in animal cruelty cases are made at the beginning, so it is crucial to know what and how to collect evidence. This requires a veterinary team to be trained and work together for a successful investigation and outcome."

The veterinary community has an obligation to the general public to identify animal abuse cases, alert the authorities, and allow the justice system to take it from there. Often veterinarians, technicians, and the animal health-care team are made aware of cases through casual client conversations, injured animals, curious circumstances, and direct communication with pet owners. In some states, veterinary teams are obligated to report animal abuse. In all instances, it is the ethical choice to report.

The American Society for Prevention of Cruelty to Animals (ASPCA) was founded in 1866, before the Society for the Prevention of Cruelty to Children. The ASPCA was formed to alleviate the injustices animals faced then, and we continue to battle cruelty today. On its extensive Web site you will find education courses and job postings and learn how to lobby for animal rights and report cruelty cases (www.aspca.org/site/PageServer?pagename=cruelty_faq).

Chapter Resources

See also resources in Chapter 1, "Preparing to Enter the Job Market," and Chapter 15, "Government Jobs."

American Association for Laboratory Animal Sciences. www.aalas.org. 1-901-754-8620. Contributes to the advancement of responsible laboratory-animal care through certification and education.

American Pet Products Manufacturers Association in America. www.appma.org. 1-203-532-0000. Promotes the interests of the industry through surveys and economic reports. It has a large membership.

AVMA Membership Directory and Resource Manual. www.avma.org. Includes current and updated addresses of many of the groups or associations listed throughout this book.

Bureau of Labor Statistics. www.bls.gov/oes/current/oes292056.htm. This Web site categorizes technician jobs into research, teaching, and more.

Industry Web sites. You can access a list of job openings at just about any company by visiting its Web site.

Pet Industry Distributors Association. www.pida.org. 1-443-640-1060.

Pet Industry Weekly blog. www.petweekly.blogspot.com. Shares pet industry news and emerging trends for dog, cat, and small-animal businesses. Features trade shows, market research, designs for pet businesses, and more.

Product Forum and Marketing News. www.vlsstore.com. Supplement to Veterinary Forum and Veterinary Technician published by Veterinary Learning Systems quarterly. Contains new product releases, technical editorials, Web site links, and contact information.

Vetguide. www.vetguide.com. Veterinary Economics supplement. Ilustrated buyers' guide to equipment and supplies with a large array of companies post their services and goods.

Veterinary Forensics

American Society for Prevention of Cruelty to Animals. www.aspca.org. 1-800-628-0028.

Merck, Melinda D. 2007a. "Veterinary Forensics." *NAVTA Journal*, Winter.

Merck, Melinda D. 2007b. *Veterinary Forensics: Animal Cruelty Investigations.* New York: Wiley Blackwell.

Sinclair, Leslie, Melinda D. Merck, and Randall Lakewood. 2006. *Investigation of Animal Cruelty: A Guide for Veterinary and Law Enforcement Professionals.* Gaithersburg, MD: Humane Society Press.

Association and Organization Jobs

There are good opportunities for technicians to work in organized veterinary medicine. *Organized veterinary medicine* is a term used by veterinarians and their teams refer to the associations that focus on professional issues. In addition to those groups with direct ties to veterinary teams, many other livestock or animal related groups may have jobs for technicians.

Associations that may hire technicians full-time include the National Association of Veterinary Technicians in America (NAVTA), the American Veterinary Medical Association (AVMA), the American Animal Hospital Association (AAHA), and some state associations. The Colorado Association of Certified Veterinary Technicians (CACVT) has had a paid administrator since 2006. Other potential employers include animal welfare organizations, the American Kennel Club (AKC), the Orthopedic Foundation for Animals (OFA, certifies dogs of certain breeds as free of signs of joint disease), the Delta Society (devoted to the human-animal bond), the National Cattlemen's Beef Association, and the Morris Animal Foundation.

These are primarily indoor jobs that include lots of telephone communication, reading, writing, supervising, and managing. Some positions require extensive travel and involve many meetings. Many allow for continual contact with veterinarian teams. Some positions that would be ideal for a technician are not necessarily advertised that way, and many times the person responsible for hiring has a standard impression of "technician" jobs and may tell you that the organization doesn't have any jobs for a "tech." Modify your approach—ask about any job openings at all, then consider whether they are suitable for your talents.

Association Director or Administator

Most associations have one or more people doing a variety of administrative work. The title *administrator* or *director* does not necessarily reflect a consistent picture of the work involved; work is divided among paid staff and elected officers in different ways within every organization. Many groups have an elected or appointed volunteer board of directors that makes decisions regarding the organization. Work can be as simple as maintaining the membership mailing list and sending out announcements or as complex as managing large meetings (in various locations or online). You can refer to published bylaws that are available on Web sites to determine how the association is structured.

Technicians can be association leaders. At least one state technician association has both an executive director and an administrator. Ivy Leventhal, CVT, applied for the administrator position of the CACVT immediately following graduation from an AVMA-accredited program. "I felt the administrator position capitalized on my talents." She splits her time between CACVT and the Colorado Veterinary Medical Foundation, focusing on the state animal response team and animal disaster relief.

Denise Mikita, MS, CVT, is the executive director of the CACVT. She has held that job since 2001 and says, "I am humbled and honored to represent the veterinary technicians in our state. I'm responsible for carrying out the directives of the executive board, committee chairs, and chapters."

Denise had always wanted to work with animals and did so for four years after graduating from an AVMA-accredited program. After working in veterinary clinics for a few years, she applied for the CACVT administrator position (at the time it was a split with the Colorado Veterinary Medical Association and Denver Area Veterinary Medical Society). She has since been given the job of executive director and has hired another certified veterinary technician (CVT) as a part-time administrator. Denise advises, "Be professional—you represent all the other people in the veterinary technician field, not just yourself. Be a good example for all."

The most rewarding aspect of her career, she says, is networking. She has the opportunity to meet with many groups in the veterinary profession. Denise has learned how to work with others and also how to benefit from their knowledge to enhance the association she works for. The most challenging part of her job is staying current on relevant issues that impact the profession. She networks with a number of different organizations, and at times it is difficult to juggle those meetings and missions. Working with great volunteers who are always coming up with new and valuable ideas for the profession drives her. Prioritizing, at times, can be a challenge.

Daily work

Day-to-day tasks include working at the computer and conducting meetings. A lot of time is spent communicating with people (group members, journalists, members of related groups) on the phone, by mail, by fax, by email, or in person at meetings. Travel is required (up to 50 percent of the time), both to conduct meetings for the association and to represent the association at various gatherings.

Pros include working with motivated and outstanding members of the profession, working on a wide variety of tasks and issues, and keeping current on important issues facing the profession. There is little contact with animals, and there are stressful times as deadlines near and conflicts arise among constituents. Working hours are well defined, although overtime and weekend work are occasionally necessary.

Organizational work dictates that you subordinate your personal opinion to the official position of the group, and you may have to work closely with people with whom you disagree on a particular issue. Meetings can become tedious, juggling many projects at once can be difficult, and the amount of time it takes to resolve issues can be frustrating. There is a need to continually adapt to newly elected officers of the association each year, which can make you feel pulled in different directions.

Pay

Salaries for these jobs vary widely, especially since this is a very new aspect of technician careers. States with a low population may hire a part-time administrator at first; as the association grows, so will the duties, pay, and benefits. Contacting your state association leaders regarding a position requires generating a well-thought-out plan, as many of the leaders may be unaware of what it takes to manage a professional association. The good news is that there are a number of people, both technicians and veterinarians, willing to help you in your research. View the Web site of the American Association of Veterinary Medical Association Executives for programs, job descriptions, and current salaries.

Qualifications/to start

Qualifications include experience in some kind of practice, excellent verbal and written communication skills, and computer literacy (ideally, Word, Excel, PowerPoint; online communication, including group meetings, webinars, sending/receiving attachments, database work; and all other aspects of group management done via distance). Administrators and directors must have an ability to work with people on complex and often controversial issues. A director must have staff management and administrative skills, usually gained by performing those tasks in private practice and by reading materials from and attending talks by practice management experts. Leadership skills are essential. The director generally lives in the city where the association or group has its headquarters. A director of a state association should have a history of working within the association in volunteer positions; the director overseeing a conference benefits from previous experience on a conference committee.

Computer skills are a must, as most associations maintain a database of members and a Web site (which must be updated periodically). The director is often the one person who works consistently with a series of elected officers; thus, the director must keep the association's history (decisions, policies) in a transferable and easily searched format. Directors also may maintain or assist with the maintenance of the association's financial records; familiarity with spreadsheets and accounting software is a plus.

Some paid directors have a background in management or are Certified Meeting Professionals (CMPs) (www.conventionindustry.org, 1-517-527-3116) or Certified Association Executives (www.asae.org, 1-269-429-0300).

To learn more, talk to technicians and veterinarians who serve on state association committees or on a board of directors. Volunteering on a board or committee is a good way to gain experience; these are part-time, volunteer positions. Once you are involved with a particular association, you will have a better idea of how to advance to a paid position.

NAVTA or State Veterinary Technician Associations

Jobs with NAVTA or your state technician association may be of interest to you. Even if a position does not currently exist, you can make a determined effort to create a new position. Most are volunteer positions, although some are paid.

NAVTA is the authorized voice for the veterinary technician profession. Its objective is to advance the science and art of veterinary medicine through programs of member service and public education. NAVTA operates through a lot of volunteer labor and sponsorships of corporations. If you volunteer, consider it a "job" that will add to your resumé and help you learn new skills.

The general membership elects new executive board members each year. The executive board consists of the immediate past president, president, president-elect, corresponding secretary, recording secretary, and two members-at-large. Terms vary. For a complete list of duties and responsibilities, view its Web site, www.navta.net. Members seek positions on different committees and task forces. NAVTA has recently reinvented itself as a leader in the veterinary community. Be sure to check the Web site for new opportunities to serve.

Pay

Andrea Ball was hired as the new executive director of NAVTA at the beginning of 2008. She is paid comparably to other directors of professional organizations with the same number of members. She receives a great benefits package and works flexible hours; her travel and expenses are paid, and she has elevated the standard of professionalism. She is prepared to hire needed part-time assistance and recently hired a communications and professional relations director, who will focus on the *NAVTA Journal* and building stronger relations within the veterinary community.

Volunteers may receive some expense reimbursement. When on an executive board, national or state, you may be reimbursed for travel expenses. Make sure you understand duties, responsibilities, and possible reimbursement options when you volunteer.

To start

Get involved! Belonging and being active in your state and national associations can be far more beneficial than you imagine. Learning about your profession from the "working side" of the association is an invaluable experience. NAVTA sponsors a leadership conference in conjunction with the Central Veterinary Conference in Kansas City. The Committee on Veterinary Technician Specialties works diligently to secure standards and reviews society applications yearly.

NAVTA publications division

The *NAVTA Journal* is produced and edited by independent contractors who work for the association (see Chapter 11, "Writing, Editing, and Publishing"). The journal is published quarterly. There are articles on veterinary technician careers and continuing education, a state report from active members, updates on classes offered around the United States, and commentary from a number of writers. The editor is a paid position. There is also an advertising component: a person who researches companies, sets up contracts for advertising, and tracks payments. The two individuals must work closely together to meet deadlines, follow up on payments, interact with a number of veterinary companies, and represent the association on a professional level at all times. There is also a journal design position.

Animal Welfare Organizations

Mindy Bough, BA, BAS, CVT, is the director of Client Services for the American Society for Prevention of Cruelty to Animals (ASPCA). Her career change has offered opportunities for advancement, not always an option in private practice. Mindy states that the most rewarding aspect of her position is being able to help others on her team to meet their goals and grow professionally.

Several national humane or animal welfare organizations employ technicians on staff, including the Humane Society of the United States, state Societies for the Prevention of Cruelty to Animals (SPCAs), and the American Humane Society. Other smaller, nongovernmental humane or animal welfare organizations may employ technicians on staff. Both administrative and hands-on animal work are possible.

Details about shelter work are found in Chapter 15, "Government Jobs," since many shelters are run by local governments.

The American Animal Hospital Association

AAHA is a group whose mission is to enhance the ability of veterinarians to provide quality medical care to companion animals and to maintain their facilities with high standards of excellence. The association certifies member veterinary hospitals if they meet stringent criteria for excellence. This organization continues to grow, and the standards they set always raise the bar in veterinary medicine.

AAHA employs both veterinarians and technicians in the field and in the office, located in Denver, Colorado. Technicians in the AAHA office assist practice consultants by coordinating on-site visits, speaking with managers to assist in the hospital-accreditation evaluation, answering questions, and enhancing the accreditation experience. The practice consultants, veterinary health-care professionals with experience as veterinary technicians or practice managers, work in various areas of the country and are responsible for AAHA's on-site hospital evaluations.

The AAHA board of directors is a group of selected volunteers who serve two-year terms. One position on the board is filled by a technician. This is a great leadership position that provides opportunities to learn and to meet with other leaders. Technicians who apply for this board position should have some experience working with other associations (e.g., as an elected officer of another group).

Daily work

Terri Johnson, CVT, BA, MSS, works in Lakewood, Colorado, at AAHA; she is a practice accreditation coordinator. She has been in the profession since 1997. "Knowing I am making a difference for people working in practice and knowing that ultimately what we do helps pets have a better life and better experience when they go to their veterinarian" are what bring Terri the most joy in her job.

Terri's senior manager is an Registered Veterinary Technician and her supervisor is a Certified Veterinary Practice Manager (see Chapter 8, "Practice Management"). Currently, there are five CVTs who work as accreditation coordinators and nine practice consultants (seven of whom are Credentialed Veterinary Technicians).

Terri also helps members prepare for their practice evaluations and coaches and supports them through the preparation process. She does research and often supplies them with the tools to succeed as an accredited AAHA hospital. Her department takes calls from members on topics ranging from controlled substances to safety and what type of flooring is recommended when building a new facility. This expertise has helped everyone in the veterinary community, beyond the immediate AAHA members.

"It is rewarding every day to be able to assist practices with problems, finding information and helping them be the best they can be by solving problems together," Terri offers. She also advises technicians to learn as much as they can, not to be afraid to ask questions, and to look for other options if they're unhappy with what they are doing.

Practice consultants live all over the United States. With the help of the practice accreditation coordinators, they visit hospitals seeking AAHA accreditation. They work out of their homes and travel to clinics in their region, visiting veterinary hospitals of all types and sizes. It is their job to physically inspect the facilities and ensure that AAHA standards are being met. They offer suggestions for improvements, speak with members of the veterinary team, review protocols, and scrutinize logs and systems in place, always elevating the practice's management. They maintain an itinerary of hospitals to be visited, write and file on-site reports, and promote association membership. Computer literacy is required. Travel (flying and driving) is a major part of the job.

Pay/qualifications

Viewing AAHA's Web site, www.aahanet.org, revealed a number of jobs available. The Career Center is very easy to navigate. Some of the not-for-profit positions were within AAHA. Within the not-for-profit category, there were eight positions listed for a veterinary technician. One was as a practice consultant in the Boston area. The pay range was $45,000 to $55,000. Requirements included being either a Credentialed Veterinary Technician or a Certified Veterinary Practice Manager with eight years of experience in the veterinary community. The applicant must be able to travel. Job descriptions are available on the Web site.

Chapter Resources

American Society of Association Executives. www.asae.org. 1-269-429-0300. Conducts association management career seminars where you can learn more about a career in association management and sponsors continuing education meetings for association executives. It certifies association executives who complete an examination and offer evidence of successful association management skills. Job search, listing openings, and salaries can be found on the site. It has a resumé critique service.

American Society of Veterinary Medical Association Executives. www.vmaexecs.org. Promotes cooperation and education among administrative executives of veterinary organizations. It publishes a newsletter, a member profile book, and a membership directory; hosts an annual public relations workshop; and holds an annual continuing education meeting.

AVMA. 2007. "Propelling the AVMA Forward." *AVMA Journal*, December 15.

Bough, Mindy. 2007. "Outside the Box Provides Exciting Opportunities." *NAVTA Journal*, Winter.

Meeting Professionals. www.mpiweb.org. 1-972-702-3000. International professionals who plan or manage meetings for associations; offers certification in Meeting Professional and Meeting Manager and offers online courses.

Tucker, Andrea Vardaro. 2007. "All About the Network: A Talk with Denise J. Mikita, MA, CVT." *Veterinary Technician Journal*, March.

Tucker, Andrea Vardaro. 2007. "Leaping to Great Heights: A Talk with Deborah B. Reeder, RVT." *Veterinary Technician Journal*, November.

International, Volunteer, and Service Work

Technicians who want to broaden their horizons, to travel, or to help others may find a niche in international, volunteer, or service work. These jobs include clinical veterinary medicine, public health, animal production and health, economics, and research. Most jobs are with government, service/assistance, and educational or religious organizations. There are likely to be openings in industry for technicians with foreign-language skills and an interest in travel. For other international positions, see Chapter 9, 12, and 15. Animal shelter jobs are discussed in Chapter 15, "Government Jobs."

Volunteering is rewarding! But why work in a low- or zero-pay job? The skills and experience you gain may fill a void in your resumé or give you that extra leg up for certain jobs. A short-term position done on the side or over vacation may also provide you with a temporary mental break from your current job without taking the leap of leaving that job. You can use the experience to reflect on your goals. And once you are on the path to achieving your life goals, you may feel, as others do, that it is time to "give back" and help others in a more permanent way as you have been helped yourself.

Associations

See Chapter 13, "Association and Organization Jobs," for details. Although a few of these positions are paid, many more are volunteer positions.

Animal Welfare Groups

Animal welfare jobs are discussed in Chapter 15, "Government Jobs," since many of these groups operate under local or state governments. However, others are managed by independent nonprofit organizations.

For a wide variety of new opportunities, search for "veterinary technician/nurse and volunteer" on the Internet. A recent search turned up an opportunity in Cozumel (go diving, then work by helping out at the humane shelter there). Veterinarians and technicians often work together in animal shelters neutering pets, and find the experience highly rewarding. Another Web site offered an opportunity to assist at the Alley Cat Guardians spay/neuter clinic in Modesto, California. Technicians are needed one Saturday a month to assist with surgery, recovery, and postoperative releases. Woodland Park Zoo in Seattle, Washington, offers an opportunity for licensed veterinary technician volunteers in their Zoo Corps. Search-and-rescue jobs are another option. Some of these are also government-run, while others are independent groups.

Therapy Dog Training

Therapy dog training has offered veterinary technicians the opportunity to work with both animals and people in a very rewarding setting. Freedom Service Dogs (www.freedomservicedogs.org) and Canine Companions for Independence (CCI; www.cci.org) hire veterinary technicians and offer volunteer opportunities. CCI, a national organization, placed its 3,000th assistance team on August 31, 2008. Under the "Careers" tab on the CCI site, you will find career positions available throughout the United States. The benefits are good and the rewards immense.

International Programs

International opportunities for both paid and volunteer work are available. Viewing SalaryExpert.com revealed many options for researching salaried positions in the for-profit and not-for-profit sectors. The Web site offered information on global salary calculations, salaries in specific regions, and cost-of-living comparisons. Remember, when researching, to refer to veterinary nurses outside the United States. Salariesreview.com has formulas for money conversions. Salary comparisons are available at www.erieri.com. This site offers comparisons of 5,000 careers in 7,000 cities.

So that the veterinary community can properly address global animal health, students from veterinary and technician programs are traveling abroad with the goal of enhancing foreign-language skills and cross-cultural experiences. The goal is that veterinarians and technicians with knowledge in international animal health will provide needed expertise in state and federal governments, in the corporate animal health industry, and as consultants to U.S. livestock operations with international markets.

International externships are being established at universities, research stations, and pharmaceutical companies with offices in other countries.

In 2007, Sandy Hass, RVT, took over the duties of the secretariat of the International Veterinary Nurses and Technicians Association (see "Chapter Resources"). The secretariat's task includes creating a newsletter, overseeing the Web site, updating the membership list, fostering communication between countries, and offering advice and information to inquirers.

International relief work

There is at least one international relief list for both veterinarians and technicians, called Vetlocums. This group uses the Internet to place announcements for technicians and nurses worldwide. The service is free. You will need to read their agreement and give them your email address and your name. View its site at www.vetlocums.com; if you require more information, contact vsupport@vetlocums.com.

Other international relief jobs are found in the variety of job banks online. Remember that Web sites can change, so Google a number of sites in your search. Vetlink Employment Services supports permanent and locum positions in the veterinary community worldwide. View Vetlink, then go to the "Ads" icon for job listings (www.vetlink.com/cgi-bin/bin/classadd).

Agencies and Organizations with International Positions

A number of organizations and agencies may have positions for veterinary technicians. Some of the jobs are not paid, but others may be. If any of the organizations sound like a good fit, use the contact information provided or an Internet search to research job openings.

Heifer Project International

Heifer Project International (HPI) (whose motto is "Ending hunger, caring for the earth") helps impoverished families worldwide become self-reliant through the gift of livestock and training in their care. To help hungry families feed themselves, HPI provides more than 22 kinds of food- and income-producing animals, as well as intensive training in community development, animal husbandry, and ecologically sound, sustainable farming. Milk, eggs, wool, draft power, and other benefits from the animals improve diets and supplement income, which pays for education, clothes, health care, and better housing. HPI requires recipients to "pass on the gift" of one or more of their animals' offspring to other needy families. This practice builds self-esteem by encouraging recipients to become donors and multiplies the benefits of the gift.

HPI has a careers posting on its Web site. Openings may be available in one of the 125 offices located around the world, with 600 office and field staff. HPI headquarters is in Little Rock, Arkansas. Some opportunities may exist to fill paid positions overseas, although the group strives to involve local people whenever possible.

In addition to paid positions, there are volunteer opportunities with HPI. You can participate in HPI's mission by volunteering at one of their three learning and livestock centers, one of the five regional offices, or the world headquarters in Little Rock. You might have the opportunity to visit an HPI project in another country as a participant in a work-study program or a study tour. Locally, you can rally a fund-raising event to purchase an animal for needy families overseas.

This is exciting work that helps people around the world. However, most jobs are not paid; the salary for paid jobs never gets very high, although the benefits are usually good and personal satisfaction is high. Visit www.heifer.org.

VetAid

VetAid is a Great Britain–based international assistance group that helps families in Africa and the United Kingdom. The potential for rewards, both professional and personal, can be significant: a positive impact on over one million of the poorest people in Africa. The salary is competitive for the nonprofit sector. Veterinary practices are encouraged to participate on a vaccine donation day in May. Funds raised during the annual Vaccine Day go to support vaccination of cattle in Kenya, Mozambique, Somalia, and Tanzania. Visit www.vetaid.org.

Peace Corps

Founded in 1961 by President John F. Kennedy, the Peace Corps is a U.S. government agency that places Americans in foreign countries that have requested Peace Corps volunteers. The three goals of the Peace Corps are to promote world peace and friendship, to help promote a better understanding of the American people by the peoples served, and to promote a better understanding of other people on the part of the American people. Peace Corps volunteers work in a variety of fields, including agriculture, community development, education, business, health, nutrition, and natural resources. They fight hunger, disease, illiteracy, poverty, and lack of opportunity around the world. The length of service, including the initial three months of training, is usually around 27 months; the Peace Corps provides all living, travel, and medical expenses during that time.

Not only has the need remained for volunteers to work in agriculture, education, forestry, health, engineering, and skilled trades but also countries are increasingly requesting help in new areas: business, the environment, urban planning, youth organizations, and teaching English for commerce and technology. Emerging democracies such as the former Soviet republics have turned to the Peace Corps for assistance for the first time. A page on its Web site is dedicated to midcareer opportunities. Using a drop-down box to identify your state, you can find a Peace Corps recruiter, information kiosk, or local office. Visit www.peacecorps.gov or call 1-800-424-8580.

United Nations volunteers

The United Nations Volunteers (UNV) program operates through the Peace Corps. It was established in 1971 by the United Nations General Assembly and is administered by the UN Development Programme. UNV is based in Bonn, Germany, and is active in more than 140 countries. In 2006, the number of volunteers reached 7,856, and 36 percent of them were women. Approximately 51 percent of UN volunteers serve in Africa, 18 percent work in Asia and the Pacific, 10 percent work in the Middle East, and about 18 percent work in Latin America.

Applicants must fill out a medical history and undergo physical and dental exams (a health condition easily managed at home can become a serious medical problem in countries the UNV serves). Host countries do not often have medical care comparable to that in the United States; sites can be remote, and often assignments are physically and emotionally challenging.

To be eligible for UNV service, you must be a U.S. citizen. There is no upper age limit; in fact, there is a 50-plus category that is very strong and growing. Married couples may serve in the UNV; both must apply and be accepted, and it is usually more difficult for the UNV to place them. Those with dependent children are not accepted. Most assignments require a bachelor's degree, some require a master's, and some require three to five years of work experience instead of or in addition to a degree. To increase your chances of acceptance, it is recommended that you apply at least six to eight months before the time you are available to depart. Contact the Peace Corps, www.peacecorps.gov, 1-800-424-8580; or United Nations Volunteers, Postfach 260 111, D-53153, Bonn, Germany; or visit www.unv.org.

Christian Veterinary Mission

Angie Miller, a Registered Veterinary Technician living in Oklahoma, has traveled to Mongolia with the Christian Veterinary Mission (CVM) three times. During her first trip, she spent five weeks teaching veterinary students English medical terminology at the University for Veterinary Medicine in Ulaanbaatar, Mongolia.

The next year, she taught small-animal terminology skills to local veterinarians in their clinics in the city. During her last visit, she coordinated a hematology class for veterinarians from all over the country. She reports that a veterinary degree in Mongolia is a five-year bachelor's degree with little hands-on training. As a credentialed veterinary technician going to a foreign country, you have an incredible amount of knowledge and many skills to offer.

"I love sharing all that I can with people who are so eager to learn. If it were possible for me to go every year, I would do it in a heartbeat! It also gives me an opportunity to share with these people the love of a wonderful God," comments Angie when asked about her experiences.

The CVM works to challenge, empower, and facilitate, serving others through their profession and living out their Christian faith. On its Web site, veterinary technicians may seek employment opportunities, view upcoming classes, and discover the many ways the veterinary community can influence cross-cultural exchanges. CVM publishes the monthly *Christian Veterinary Journal*, filled with challenging articles, compelling photos, and highlights of the work being done by CVM in the United States and abroad. The current director is a veterinarian. Visit www.cvmusa.org or call 1-206-546-7201.

Rotary Club International

Rotary was founded for the purpose of exchanging information with people in diversified careers, fellowship, and community service. It quickly spread into international service. Rotary's group exchanges are small groups of young professional and business people in their twenties (typically four people plus an older Rotarian leader). A four to six week exchange is arranged with a similar group from another part of the world, with an intensive schedule of visits involving many talks and presentations. Candidates for the program are recruited by the local Rotary clubs and sponsored by the district.

Rotary clubs enhance their communities by striving to meet the credo "Service Above Self," the foundation of club activity. Vocational service includes club members serving others through their professions and aspiring to high ethical standards. Disaster relief and recovery have been a primary focus, aiding victims of disaster and fostering humanitarian efforts. According to a Rotary member: "Some of our scholarship recipients study veterinary science abroad, and some of the professionals who participate in our exchanges are vets. There have been some grants to developing countries to provide or improve care of livestock." Visit www.rotary.org or call 1-847-866-3000.

World Health Organization and Pan American Health Organization

The World Health Organization (WHO) and the Pan American Health Organization (PAHO) continually seek the services of highly qualified health professionals. The professional technical staff act as advisers in public health to member governments and, consequently, candidates must possess substantial training and experience in this field before they can be considered for an assignment.

PAHO was established in 1902; in 1948, it was franchised by WHO as its regional office for the Americas. It serves as the specialized agency in health for the Organization of the American States and the United Nations. Within PAHO, the Veterinary Public Health Program is under the Division of Disease Prevention and Control. This is a large, unique program with a worldwide staff of more than 200. Viewing the Web site, www.paho.org, under the "UN Vacancy" tab, revealed jobs available in Barbados; Washington, D.C.; Ecuador; and Jamaica. Most of the professional staff are Doctors of Veterinary Medicine; however, technicians may be suitable for positions if they hold postgraduate degrees and work experience in preventive medicine and public health. General service staff need communication skills, preferably are bilingual with a third language desirable, and possess a business background and computer skills. Applications are found online at the WHO Web site under "Employment."

Job requirements vary depending on the position, but typically an advanced degree in public health is highly valued. In addition, most adviser positions require at least seven years of experience at the national level and at least two years of participation in technical cooperation programs and activities, preferably in the American Legion for posts stationed in the Americas. PAHO positions normally require fluency in English and Spanish. Knowledge of Portuguese and French is desirable. Language requirements are specified for each vacancy. Local recruitment in the general services category had openings for technical assistants in Switzerland, the Philippines, and Kyrgyzstan. A technical officer in epidemiology was needed in Cairo, Egypt.

Visit WHO/PAHO at www.paho.org or info@who.int. Note that due to the high volume of queries received, an individual response may not be possible.

Other overseas opportunities

A wide variety of service and church groups may provide opportunities for short-term international work. Contact those in your area for more information.

Write to veterinary technician (nurse) programs in countries of interest and ask if there are any courses, internships, or volunteer opportunities. For instance, National University Ireland graduated its first class of veterinary nurses in June 2004. The World Small-Animal Veterinary Association (WSAVA, www.wsava.org, info@wasava.org) has listings of a few veterinary nursing programs. WSAVA sponsors an annual continuing education conference. Veterinary nurses/ technicians are invited to attend the classes. You may be interested in attending to broaden your networking, travel abroad, and acquire continuing education credits— what a deal! Contact the secretariat of the International Veterinary Nurse and Technicians Association (www.ivnta.org or info@ivnta.org) for questions. Its Web site is limited; however, the secretariat may have access to more international networking opportunities. The British Veterinary Nursing Association's Web site (www.bvna. org.uk) offers free job postings and locum announcements. The Veterinary Nurses Council of Australia (www.vnca.asn.au) and the Veterinary Nurses Association of South Africa (www.vnasa.co.za, info@vnasa.co.za) may lead to contacts in those countries. Vetlink Employment Services (www.vetlink.com) identifies jobs in general practice, industry, and government around the world. Initial contacts may be for gathering information; who knows where your inquisitive questioning may take you?

The Organization of American States (OAS) Student Intern Program is designed for junior and senior high school students and graduate students at the university level to allow them to work within their fields of study. The experience has given students a great opportunity, expanding their international organization skills while enhancing their self-esteem and personal capabilities. Scholarships are available; however, the intern program is unpaid. A 3.0 GPA is required, along with a weeklong teaming with senior officials of the OAS. Visit www.oas.org or call 1-202-458-3000.

You can get information about many groups through InterAction, a coalition of over 150 U.S.-based nonprofits that promote human dignity and development in 165 countries around the world. In the United States, these groups are called "private and voluntary organizations," or PVOs. InterAction coordinates and promotes these human development activities and helps to ensure that goals are met in an ethical and cost-efficient manner. Internships are offered in six different areas: office of the president, finance and administration, communications, human-itarian policy and practice, membership and standards, and public policy. These programs are available for undergraduate students with interests in finance and nonprofit organizations. Interns have an opportunity to work with leading profes-sionals in humanitarian organizations and government agencies. Disaster response, avian flu, and animal health are venues in which veterinary technicians may assist InterAction in reaching its goals of humanitarian development around the world. Visit www.interaction.org or call 1-202-667-8227.

When approaching any of these groups, you may be turned down when you ask about positions for veterinary technicians/nurses. Instead, start by asking about positions related to agriculture, animal disaster relief, or livestock management.

Chapter Resources

See resources in Chapter 9, "Consulting"; Chapter 12, "Careers in the Veterinary 'Industry'"; and Chapter 15, "Government Jobs."

Animal Welfare

American Society for the Prevention of Cruelty to Animals. www.aspca.org. 1-800-628-0028.

Humane Society of the United States. www.hsus.org. 1-202-452-1100.

Search Dog Foundation. www.searchdogfoundation.org/98/html/1_be_handler.html. 1-888-459-4376.

Therapy Dogs

Canine Companions for Independence. www.cci.org. 1-800-572-2275.

The Delta Society. www.deltasociety.org. Has information about becoming involved in animal-assisted activities.

Delta Society's Pet Partners Program. www.deltasociety.org/VolunteerAboutFaq.htm. 1-425-679-5500. Trains volunteers and screens volunteers and their pets for visiting-animal programs in hospitals, nursing homes, rehabilitation centers, schools, and other facilities.

Fine, A. 2006. *Handbook on Animal-Assisted Therapy: Theoretical Foundations and Guidelines for Practice.* Chandler, AZ: Academic Press.

Freedom Service Dogs. www.freedomservicedogs.org. 1-303-922-6231.

Whitehouse, Bernard S. 1995. *Animal-Assisted Therapy: A Guide for Health Care Professionals and Volunteers.* White House, TX: Therapet.

International Work

International Veterinary Nurses and Technicians Association. www.ivnta.org. info@ivnta.org. Seeks to foster and promote links with veterinary nurses and technicians worldwide through communication and cooperation. Countries include Australia, Canada, Japan, New Zealand, Norway, South Africa, United Kingdom, and United States.

Kohls, L. Robert. 2001. *Survival Kit for Overseas Living for Americans Planning on Living and Working Abroad,* Fourth Edition. Boston: Nicholas Brealey Publishing in association with Intercultural Press.

Organization of American States Student Intern Program. www.oas.org. 1-202-458-3754.

Pan American Health Organization. www.paho.org. info@who.int. Shares health topics, research, and scientific writing. It has a veterinary public health unit. Note that due to the high volume of queries received, an individual response may not be possible.

Peace Corps. www.peacecorps.gov. 1-800-424-8580.

Rabe, Monica. 1997. *Culture Shock! A Practical Guide to Living and Working Abroad.* London: Kuperard, Times Editions Pte Ltd.

Rhinestine, Stephen. 1996. *Manager's Guide to Globalization: Six Skills for Success in a Changing World.* Columbus, OH: McGraw-Hill. More recent books written by Rhinestine are also available.

United Nations Volunteers. www.unv.org. Information@unvolunteers.org. General inquiries are encouraged; contact them via email.

Vetlink Employment Services. www.vetlink.com. Has offices in Melbourne, Perth, and contacts in United Kingdom, Canada, and New Zealand. Locum and permanent positions are available.

World Health Organization. www.who.int. Has a job vacancy tab; start with "Scientist," then "Veterinarian," and then "Veterinary Technician/Nurse."

Government Jobs

What does "working for the government" mean to you? The reality of government work is far more varied than you may think. These jobs pay well, offer intellectual stimulation, and can fill your needs for working with animals, if you so desire.

Government Jobs

This chapter discusses general information about all government, followed by specific agencies and the jobs within them. The exact job descriptions may change, but the general ideas remain the same. Be patient reading this chapter; understanding specific job descriptions requires a discussion of each agency's organizational structure. If you can wade through that, then you've passed criteria necessary for government jobs.

One important area of government jobs is animal shelter work. Shelters are often city- or county-funded, although they may also operate as nonprofit groups. These jobs include small-animal, equine, and food-animal work; hands-on animal work; laboratory and research work; and management or supervisory positions.

When considering government jobs, remember to look beyond jobs that require higher degrees to those that simply ask for someone with a science background, or someone with a degree in microbiology, biology, or chemistry. Think of your overall qualifications, not just your degrees; for example, you write well, have held supervisory positions, and have dealt with the public.

Daily work

Benefits of any government job include good pay and great benefits, raises, fairly regular hours, and a clear job description (i.e., you know what you're supposed to be doing). Field jobs allow you to continue to work with livestock and with ranchers and farmers, without many practice headaches (the type of animals you'll work with depends on the state; e.g., pigs in Iowa, cattle in Montana). Jobs can be located in rural or urban areas. Sometimes you can travel to interesting places. Once you learn the policies and procedures, you can focus on the more interesting parts of your job, whether that be pathology (food inspection), disease management, animal care, or herd health (alongside a veterinarian). Pay varies from position to position and can depend on whether you are working for the city, state, or federal government. Typically, though, benefits are good, as is job security.

Government veterinarians need to care about regulations (which most do, since they understand the reasons behind the rules), and it is in the veterinary technician's best interest to know the laws that govern both animal welfare and the veterinary profession. Technicians working with government veterinarians must be able to write well and to complete reports. Travel is often required.

Any job descriptions or titles listed here may be changed, so consult each agency for up-to-date information. However, the descriptions here should give you a good idea of the types of work involved.

Working for City Government

Cities throughout the United States hire veterinary technicians for positions in public health, animal shelters, or animal-care facility inspections. Recently the American Veterinary Medical Association (AVMA) and the American Medical Association (AMA) adopted the One Health Initiative, in which veterinary technicians can play a vital role, collaborating on health issues that cross both the human and the animal medical fields, including pandemic influenza, bioterrorism risks, and biomedical research. This new initiative will unfold over the next decade, offering numerous opportunities for the technician. The majority of veterinary technician jobs in government are with animal shelters. Veterinarians do most animal-care facility inspections.

City or county public health

Cities and counties have public health departments that may hire veterinary technicians. Contact your city or county public health department for information about specific positions and their titles.

Animal shelter veterinary technician

Many animal shelters hire a full-time staff veterinarian. Some shelters do not hire Doctors of Veterinary Medicine at all, while others retain a DVM only on a part-time or consulting basis. Still others contract with a veterinary hospital to perform necessary procedures such as spay and neuter surgery. Veterinary technicians often work closely with nearby hospitals, veterinarians, and animal control, assessing cases and animal behavior.

The shelter technician assists with basic medical and surgical procedures on shelter animals, vaccinates, assists with spays and neuters, identifies animals with a tattoo or microchip, and euthanizes. Long-term or complex care is usually not performed, since resources must be concentrated on those animals most likely to be adopted. Life-saving medical care, but not extensive care, is given to injured animals. Shelter technicians are often called upon during disaster situations, and they must be ready to handle large numbers of animals, if necessary. They are often in charge of investigating claims of animal abuse. Veterinary technicians must be especially knowledgeable about animal behavior problems, disease transmission, and kennel management. Making public presentations (e.g., speaking to school-children and other groups about pet ownership), serving as a liaison with related groups, and working with the local veterinary medical association to decide what medical and surgical care should be performed by the shelter staff versus private practices may all be done by a shelter technician. There is also potential to move up to a shelter management position.

According to Lizann Risk, human resources manager of the Humane Society of Boulder Valley, Colorado:

> Traditionally, animal shelters are known for promoting from within. As shelter workers become proficient in handling animals, understanding herd health, comprehending the importance of animal flow through the building, and assessing health/behavior, they are often tapped to advance within the organization. These days, progressive organizations look for "soft skills" required to manage people. When I hire for a manager or supervisor, I look for experience in managing people; the ability to conduct a difficult conversation; ability to manage change/transition; demonstrated skills in managing a budget and/or resources; and creativity, initiative, and critical thinking.

Daily work

The shelter veterinary technician performs a needed public service and promotes responsible pet ownership. Parts of the job can be intellectually challenging, including kennel management and working within a political structure. Cons include repetitive surgical work, performing or witnessing many euthanasias, constraints of a limited budget, inability to treat and follow through on complex cases, and sometimes a bad reputation among local hospitals. Overcoming the idea that shelters compete with hospitals may be the most difficult challenge. This may be diminished through networking, educating, and bridge building. Hours are fairly regular, although the shelter technician may have to take emergency calls during evenings and weekends.

The National Animal Control Association published a list of "pros and cons of working in the field of animal control." Pros included the joy of seeing animals adopted by loving, responsible people; the gratification of ensuring that impounded animals are provided with shelter and care; the peace of knowing that unwanted animals are at least given a humane and dignified death; the excitement of unusual animal calls; and the friendships developed with other shelter workers all over the country. Cons included frustrations with irresponsible pet owners; lack of understanding by the public of the need for animal control and of problems of animal overpopulation; stress from abuse by people; depression because of animal euthanasia; exposure to communicable disease and injuries by animals and humans; and sometimes long hours or being on call.

Pay

Pay varies by geographic area but is generally as good as that of the average veterinary technician employed in private practice. The benefits are excellent. For example, one large city offers full medical and dental benefits, a retirement plan, professional memberships, insurance, license fees, and more.

Qualifications

Most positions require only an associate's of applied science degree, but others may require management; public speaking; organizational, administrative, or fundraising skills; and knowledge of animal behavior and kennel management.

To add to your expertise, find out whether your local community college offers classes in human relations, city management, municipal law, or public relations. Read the literature about animal behavior. Join Toastmasters if you have trouble speaking in public.

To start

Most cities have an animal control department or neighborhood services. Call your local department to learn particulars. You may also see job ads in the publications of the associations listed below, in local newspapers, on the city's Web page, and in veterinary journals. (See Chapter 13, "Association and Organization Jobs.")

Colorado Mountain College offers an animal shelter management certificate of occupational proficiency that requires a minimum of 20 credits. Many of the requisite courses are part of the veterinary technology degree; others are in the areas of business management, accounting, and human relations. There is a work experience course as well, during which the student spends 135 total hours at two different shelters. More specific information can be found at www.coloradomtn.edu/programs/vet/animal-shelter/home.shtml or the central services office number, 1-800-621-8559.

Sample Job Announcement *(Found on www.indeed.com)*

Position Description: Essential functions include: monitoring the general health of shelter animals and checking for injuries, signs of illness or unusual behavior, conducting basic physical screening exams and providing for treatment according to pre-established guidelines; rendering emergency treatment, first aid and follow-up care to all animals in need; providing care and treatment to alleviate problems detrimental to impounded animals' health and well-being; administering prescribed medications and inoculations; assisting the veterinarian in surgery and ensuring that all equipment and instruments are at hand, operable, and sanitized; performing a variety of diagnostic procedures, including collecting samples for analysis, taking and developing X-rays, and conducting laboratory tests; maintaining inventory of all pharmaceuticals, equipment, and supplies; providing care and feeding to animals in vet room; performing euthanasia of animals in accordance with established laws and departmental policy; maintaining accurate and legible case files and records; using a computer to input, update, and access information regarding shelter animals and to produce written documents; providing information and responding to inquiries from the public; assisting in instructing shelter staff in proper care and feeding of a wide variety of animals, basic animal health practices and procedures, and signs of common health problems; screening animals for suitability for adoption; performs related duties as assigned.

Minimum Qualifications: One year of experience working with a variety of animals in an animal shelter, kennel, or veterinary hospital facility.

Willingness Checklist: As part of the application process, all applicants must complete a willingness checklist. This document lists examples of essential functions and required working conditions encountered by a 3375 Animal Health Technician.

Animal-care facility inspection

This job involves inspecting facilities where animals are raised or cared for, such as dog-breeding kennels, veterinary clinics, veterinary technician programs, research facilities with laboratory animals, and horse protection. State laws or city ordinances define which facilities are to be inspected and by whom. In some states and cities, there is no provision for inspection of veterinary hospitals. In some cities, a shelter DVM is also responsible for animal facility inspection. See the federal government, APHIS/Animal Welfare section, for a description of animal-care jobs, then contact your government agencies to find out who is responsible for carrying out those duties where you live. United States Department of Agriculture–Animal and Plant Health and Inspection Service–Animal Welfare has three offices in the United States. Visit www.aphis.usda.gov/animal_welfare or call 1-301-734-7833 for more information. In recent years, employee training in this area has increased, as animal welfare and critical enforcement needs are redefined and laws are becoming more stringent.

Working for the State Government

In general, state positions for veterinary technicians focus on public health, control of livestock disease, and zoonosis. Advancement to managerial and administrative positions is possible. The main employment opportunities are with the departments of public health and agriculture.

State departments of health are mainly concerned with human health. As all veterinary technicians know, this is directly related to animal health through the food supply and zoonotic disease. State departments of agriculture are primarily concerned with animal disease control. Since this can directly affect human health, there can be significant overlap among job duties. Job titles for veterinary technicians vary by state. Some states will put the department of health in charge of a certain area, whereas other states put their department of agriculture in charge of that very same area. Examples of this potential overlap include a variety of food programs, such as milk or egg programs or organic foods certification. Although most jobs with the words *public health* in the title are found in the public health department, there are exceptions.

Jobs for veterinary technicians exist within each state's department of agriculture. The most obvious are in the state veterinarian's office. If there is a veterinarian in a department, there may be need for a veterinary technician to work alongside the veterinarian.

State departments of public health

Veterinary technicians have fantastic opportunities in various divisions of state departments of health, which hire a wide variety of scientists.

As with federal jobs, the best advice is this: take any job with the state that you can get, and then you will find a wealth of other job opportunities that may not be obvious to the outsider. Also, once you're employed, you can educate others about the qualifications of Certified Veterinary Technicians (CVTs) that make them ideal for jobs they might not have been considered for in the past. Another tip: states with small budgets and low populations are more likely to hire CVTs for jobs with titles like toxicologist or epidemiologist, even if the applicant doesn't have a toxicology or epidemiology degree, because these states rarely have the funds to hire specialists. Once you've gained experience, you can move on to a state with a larger budget, with experience on your resumé. Jobs may focus on radiation safety, toxicology, epidemiology, and many more areas. Technicians interested in focusing on one aspect of their training might like this work. Others may take a job with a narrow focus as a springboard to other jobs.

Agriculture Research Service

The National Animal Disease Center (NADC) is part of the USDA's Agriculture Research Service (ARS). The NADC has positions in a variety of scientific disciplines, including biochemistry, immunology, physiology, virology, bacteriology, pathology, molecular biology, and veterinary medicine. There are also jobs in a variety of other areas, including animal care, facilities, budgeting, travel, human resources, procurement, secretarial, visual services, computer services, and library.

The NADC actively employs students through the school year. Employment of students is governed by research project needs and available funding. Summer intern and summer apprentice positions are also a possibility.

Daily work

Daily work varies widely, as there are a variety of positions you could fill, from administrative to research assistant. Research technician jobs can involve working outdoors and/or indoors, depending on the research topic. Administrative and clerical jobs are indoors at a desk. Search the government jobs Web site for the Agricultural Research Service to read specific job descriptions, focusing on those that say "technician" (these will be any kind of technician, not just veterinary technician jobs).

To start

Look for job advertisements in each state's personnel division; the easiest way to find listings is to look on the state's Web site or contact the department by telephone or mail. Apply for any job that involves the subjects you studied in technician school, and be ready to convey how much you know. To subscribe to a weekly listing of new vacancies within ARS, go to www.ars.usda.gov/careers/docs.htm?docid=1358, or email careers@ars.usda.gov to request the phone number for an office near you.

Cooperative extension

The Cooperative State Research, Education, and Extension Service (CREES or CSREES) is an education network based at 74 of the nation's land-grant universities. In your online search, extension agencies are listed under "County Government." Extension agents work in most counties of each state. You may have heard of the job "extension educator." Technicians may have the background to fulfill the requirements of this job.

Extension educators are basically information sources with a broad range of duties. They provide educational and technical assistance in livestock and crop production, family life, and community development. They may provide information about subjects such as home economics, cooking and canning, sewing, growing fruit, raising and caring for a variety of animals, and planting and harvesting a variety of crops.

Extension personnel serve the community in which they are located, so the range of services provided may vary with the nature of that community, usually at the county or regional level. Expect to find extension advisers who reflect the agricultural production of a community—for example, if there is a lot of dairy farming, there will probably be more dairy specialists. If you want to work in a particular area (e.g., with horses), then you'll want to apply for an extension job in a county or state where the economy depends on that sector (e.g., Kentucky).

Daily work

A new extension agent may be asked to do a community needs survey to find what needs exist and what programs are desired. The agent's job is then to deliver the information by researching it, teaching classes, finding volunteer teachers who are knowledgeable in the subject, or providing printed information. Organizing, writing, and distributing educational materials on a variety of subjects are part of the job. Much of this work is available on the Internet.

Extension educators respond to calls from community members and provide the information or assistance they need. They also conduct or organize classes on a variety of subjects. Collaborative relationships are established with county commissioners, 4-H leaders, state universities, schools, organizations, and other agencies. The amount of administrative work varies but is typically 15 percent of the total job duties.

A typical winter day in northern states is spent indoors. Summer days include lots of outdoor work with 4-H activities. Extension agents may coordinate 4-H programs, publicize the information they offer, and distribute it by phone, email, or mail. Agents may create newsletters and organize meetings with various groups. Time is often spent on the phone coordinating educational presentations, locating someone to write articles for the newsletter, and answering questions from county residents or employees.

Most extension agents have assistants, who may be administrative or 4-H program assistants. They also train local volunteers, who train others (examples include master gardeners, master food safety advisers, and master dairy goat farmers). The educator recruits, screens, trains, and counsels volunteers who help develop and implement these programs after determining program needs.

Extension agents may help coordinate animal emergency response teams, working closely with local emergency managers, state teams, and federal disaster agencies. Each county extension service is part of the county organization as well as the state network of extension agents.

As an extension agent, you'll still have contact with animals and animal lovers, without the need to be on call or to manage a business. Hours can be long. You'll be required to keep current on your medical knowledge, and you'll be able to learn more about other subjects, broadening your knowledge base. This is a very people-oriented job, working with all ages, including schoolchildren.

Pay

Pay is adequate but not high, with good benefits. SalaryExpert.com provides salary data for an agent or assistant with similar duties and educational background. Salaries range from $26,000 to $35,000, depending upon region, duties, and qualifications.

Qualifications

An agriculture background is necessary, and a background in education and development is helpful or required, depending upon the position. The area's economic base will determine the amount of time spent using knowledge of livestock or horses versus working in areas like home economics, orchard or pasture management, or gardening. Applicants with proficiency in many areas are the most likely to be hired. Emphasis is on people skills, computer and distance education skills, communication skills, and the subject matter directly pertinent to the specific opening. Teaching and administrative experience and experience working with the news media are desired. The extension agent must have effective speaking, writing, and listening skills, experience working with groups and individuals, and the ability to work independently or as a team member.

To start

There is no central employment process for extension jobs; they are advertised and filled differently by each state. When searching for job announcements, enter "university cooperative extension agent" plus the name of the state in your search engine. The state government site may have a listing under "Extension Agent" or in the general employment section. Some positions may require clerical skills. As in most cases, getting your foot in the door is an advantage in the long term and an opportunity to broaden your experience.

Working for the Federal Government: Civilian Jobs

Federal jobs can be divided into two broad categories: the uniformed and the civil services. Veterinarians have filled positions within the federal government in many departments; there may be positions for veterinary technicians under the supervision of those veterinarians or in those departments.

There is much talk about how the emphasis on global security may create new jobs. It's tough to predict in which agencies veterinarians and technicians may serve. The Department of Homeland Security (DHS) is a relatively new department. Its purpose is to coordinate the efforts of numerous agencies. Now under the auspices of the DHS are agencies such as FEMA (emergency management) and the TSA (transportation security). The Directorate for Science and Technology (www.dhs.gov/xabout/structure/editorial_0530.shtm) is the primary research and development arm of the DHS. It includes the Chemical and Biological Division. Look it up at www.dhs.gov or call 1-202-282-8000.

Daily work

Daily work varies widely, as there are a variety of positions you could fill, from administrative to research assistant. Search the government jobs Web site to read specific job descriptions, focusing on those that say "technician" (these will be any kind of technician, not just veterinary technician jobs).

Qualifications

Qualifications vary with the job, and there are government jobs for people with many qualifications. However, your chances of getting a job that pays well are greater if you have a college degree. To get an idea of the kinds of qualifications desired, search the federal government jobs Web site for "technician" and read the details for those jobs.

Federal Agencies That Employ Veterinarians and Support Teams

Department of Agriculture (USDA) includes:
Food Safety and Inspection Service (FSIS)
Agriculture Research Service (ARS)
Office of Risk Assessment and Cost-Benefit Analysis (ORACBA)
Animal and Plant Health Inspection Service (APHIS) includes:
Center for Veterinary Biologics
Centers of Epidemiology and Animal Health
National Animal Health Policy and Programs
National Center for Animal Health Emergency Management
National Center for Animal Health Programs
National Center for Import and Export

Department of Health and Human Services (DHHS) includes:
Public Health Service (PHS) includes:
Food and Drug Administration (FDA) includes:
Center for Veterinary Medicine (CVM)
Centers for Disease Control and Prevention (CDC)
National Institutes of Health (NIH)

Department of the Interior includes:
Fish and Wildlife Service (FWS)

Department of Commerce includes:
National Marine Fisheries Service (NMFS)
National Marine Mammal Laboratory (NMML)

Pay

Government worker pay is rated on a "GS scale." There are 15 GS levels and a senior executive service; at each level are several steps of pay. Recent college graduates usually enter federal service at grade GS-5 or GS-7. View www.allfederaljobs. com for a list of pay scales at each government level. When evaluating pay for federal government jobs, be sure to include the value of benefits before you compare salaries with other niches. Multiply your expected salary by 25 percent (the value of benefits) to get a comparison value. Salaries are also based on location (cost of living). For instance, a GS-7 position pays $36,783 in Atlanta, while the same position pays $41,367 in San Francisco because of the difference in cost of living.

Advancement to the next higher pay rate (step increase) is attained based on satisfactory job performance. In addition, Congress authorizes cost-of-living salary increases to keep federal pay competitive with the private sector. Employees may also be promoted (by meeting full performance and qualifications requirements) to higher levels on their career ladder. Some promotions may require a change to a different job with a different career ladder—for example, from a field position to a management position.

In addition to pay, you get great benefits: paid vacation, sick leave, and holidays; health and life insurance options; and a retirement plan. Don't forget to include these when comparing government jobs with other jobs—benefits are expensive! You can get the current GS pay chart on the Office of Personnel Management Web site or at any employment office.

Sample Job Announcement *(Found on www.usajobs.gov)*

Job Title: Food Inspector, USDA, FSIS

Salary Range: $31,315.00 to $50,431.00 per year

Many Vacancies: Location negotiable after selection, United States.

Key Requirements: U.S. citizenship; the equivalent of at least one year of full-time specialized experience, which may include, but is not limited to, the following examples of work experience.

Veterinary Technician: Conducting lab tests, assessing animals and/or partial examination of animals, performing necropsies, monitoring animals under anesthesia, and administering medications.

To start

Many federal employees will tell you the first step to take in investigating any civilian federal job is to apply for one. Just get started. This does not obligate you in any way, but it speeds up the hiring process by placing you on the eligibility list. There are two approaches to applying for federal jobs: (1) make a general application for agriculture jobs throughout the USDA-FSIS and USDA-APHIS, and (2) search the federal job listings via the Internet (www.usajobs.gov) and apply for specific job openings with specific agencies.

Consider using both approaches and then make choices based on the jobs that look interesting, and that you are qualified for based on your past experience and skills. Federal jobs are very competitive. The more jobs you apply for, the better your chances of getting one. Get your foot in the door at an entry-level position, then gain experience and develop your skills on the job. You'll notice that federal jobs are assigned numbers to identify the level and title. Don't worry about these—instead focus on duties, skills, agency, and the type of job you want.

If you want a federal job, you should consider accepting the first one available, even though it may not be your first choice. Many other federal positions will still be open to you, and many are filled by promotion as employees gain experience and qualify for higher-level jobs. Consider a summer or temporary position to gain experience that you may be lacking.

Here's what to do: Submit an application to (1) FSIS, (2) APHIS, and (3) the address on any specific job announcements you find through your federal job search (see details about each agency that follow). That approach will allow you to be considered for the largest number of job openings. Remember, you can always turn down a job offer, but you can't accept one that you never see.

Once your application is sent in, your eligibility is rated and you are placed on a list of candidates who are contacted as vacancies occur. You will have more potential job offers if you list a wide range of geographic areas in which you'd accept work, but you have the option of placing limits on both the location and the number of hours that you will work. Doing so means that you will not be contacted for any jobs that don't meet your stated limitations, so be careful with the limits you set.

Applying for nonveterinary jobs

Contact the individual agency, as described earlier. When considering a government job, remember to look beyond jobs that require an associate's in applied science degree or bachelor's of science degree to those that simply ask for someone with a science background. Think of your overall qualifications, not only your degree: you write well, give public presentations, and have supervisory experience and management skills. When filling out your application, don't limit your notes to only medical and technical areas. Include your experience or classes you have taken in management, public speaking, writing, and so on.

The easiest way to get an overview of a job is to call the recorded job vacancy phone numbers (1-202-606-252 and follow prompts) or go to the federal Office of Personnel Management's Web site at www.opm.gov (general inquiries, 1-202-606-1800). Not all vacancies are automatically listed; you should check each agency's job announcements. View www.usajobs.gov for federal jobs. Search by titles (i.e., animal caretaker, animal health technician) and locations (city, state).

Federal Government Job Categories

Veterinary technicians may be hired to work for the federal government in these areas of interest:

- Biological science
- Consumer safety
- Educator/teaching
- Fish and wildlife
- Fishery biology
- Food compliance/regulation
- Food inspection
- Food technology
- Genetics
- Health physics
- Health science (epidemiology)
- Husbandry (animal science)
- Microbiology
- Occupational safety and health (biosafety)
- Pharmacology
- Physical science
- Physiology
- Public health
- Technical writing
- Toxicology
- Veterinary medicine
- Wildlife biology
- Zoology

Transportation Security Administration

The Canine Breeding and Development Center of the Transportation Security Administration (TSA) hires a few veterinary technicians. Program specialist Diana L. Thomas says:

> The program manager and I are former vet techs. We are also dog trainers. I have been a K-9 police officer as well. Being a vet tech is not mandatory in our positions, but it has helped tremendously in our line of work. Having a background in canine reproduction and health was necessary for both of us to get our positions working with the breeding program. The DHS (Domestic Homeland Security) Canine Breeding and Development Center has a geneticist, reproductive vet, internal Med Vet, and an RVT assigned to the program. Assigned to the DHS National Explosives Detection Canine Team Program

(NEDCTP) at HQ, we have 47 K-9 trainers and evaluators, who rely on the veterinarians and technicians to take care of all medical issues. The NEDCTP has roughly 500 handlers nationwide; I am only aware of a few handlers that have had technician experience. Being a veterinary technician is obviously not mandatory, but it would surely help them to get a position as a K-9 handler with TSA, and it would without doubt help them once they are in the field working with their K-9s.

Working for the Federal Government: Military Jobs

Veterinary technicians may work for the military as enlisted members or as civilians. Most jobs are with the army, since this branch includes the veterinary corps. You may even receive your veterinary technician training after you enlist! You can then remain in the military or transfer those skills to other jobs once you have served your term of duty.

Technicians can also fill civilian jobs (within the military) as animal health technicians that are posted at www.usajobs.gov. These jobs are highly desired and have low turnover. Benefits are excellent, including vacation, health, and vision care and more. A recent search of the site revealed several positions in Hawaii, Korea, and Florida.

Sample Job Announcement

Animal Health Technician

Fort Shafter, Veterinary Treatment Facility. The Applicant is expected to perform duties of a veterinary technician; a certified veterinary technician is preferred. Duties include but are not limited to: basic examination and vaccination of pets... Agency: U.S. Army Medical Command; Location: Fort Shafter, Hawaii; Salary: $10.81 to $12.00 / Per Hour, plus benefits.

Temporary jobs with the federal government

Temporary jobs include paid and volunteer work during disasters. The National Animal Health Emergency Response Corps (NAHERC) and the National Veterinary Response Team (NVRT), for instance, operate under the federal government. Both teams consist of private citizens who have been approved as intermittent federal employees and are activated in the event of a disaster. See the

"Emergency Management" link at www.aphis.usda.gov/animal_health, as well as the "Medical Preparedness" link at www.phe.gov/preparedness/support. Disaster relief is also coordinated by professional associations. The AVMA's Veterinary Medical Assistance Teams (VMATs) serve as first responders during disasters and emergencies. These teams bridge the gaps among local, state, and national disaster programs. When requested by a state, VMAT volunteers provide operational emergency response programs. See www.avma.org/vmat.

Chapter Resources

See also resources in Chapter 13, "Association and Organization Jobs."

Animal Shelter

American Humane Association. www.animalhumanesociety.org. 1-763-522-4325. Offers classes on shelter management, compassion fatigue, and other educational programs.

American Society for the Prevention of Cruelty to Animals. www.aspca.org. 1-800-628-0028.

ASPCA's Meet Your Match Program. www.aspca.org/adoption/meet-your-match. Widely used in animal shelters to evaluate suitability of dogs for adoption. The assessment has helped animal welfare professionals nationwide identify potential aggression and opportunities for behavior modification; this ultimately leads to more adoptions through appropriate placement.

Association of Shelter Veterinarians. www.sheltervet.org.

Humane Society of the United States. www.hsus.org.

National Animal Control Association. www.nacanet.org. 1-913-768-1319.

Extension Work

Chronicle of Higher Education. www.chronicle.com. 1-202-452-1033. A national weekly tabloid of education jobs and opportunities, often including extension service positions. It also lists meetings, seminars, workshops, and classified advertising.

Cooperative State Research Education and Extension Service. www.crees.usda.gov. 1-202-720-4423. Aims to improve economic, environmental, and social conditions in the United States and globally. Select "Contact Us" for a listing of offices and general information.

County Extension Service offices. Are listed in the government section of the phone book under "County," then under "Cooperative Extension." Extension agents are hired by the state's land grant university.

Federal Government

AVMA Membership Directory and Resource Manual. www.avma.org. 1-800-248-2862. Contains lists of officials in charge of animal disease control, state public health veterinarians, officials in charge of state meat inspection, and USDA and U.S. Department of Health and Human Services offices.

Career Connection America, Government Jobs Central. www.iccweb.com. govjobs@aol.com. Very comprehensive site with information on interviewing, determining eligibility, descriptions, links to 900 jobs, and more.

Federal Career Opportunities, Federal Research Service. www.fedjobs.com. 1-800-822-5027. A free monthly email can be sent to you. Each issue contains articles on the federal hiring process. This information is available free from various government sources, but you might find it easier to read in one publication.

Federal Information Center. www.cftech.com. Call to find any government phone number; view the Web site to find phone numbers for 35 state offices.

Federal Information Exchange (FEDIX). www.fedix.fie.com. Provides electronic access to federal research and education opportunities: research, equipment grants, current events, and minority opportunities. Sponsored by several agencies.

Federal jobs. www.usajobs.gov. Visit the Web site to apply for a federal job.

Federal Research Service. www.fedjobs.com. 1-800-822-5027. A private group specializing in helping people get government jobs. It has a lot of resources, including a newsletter and *Federal Career Opportunities*, with an extensive, up-to-date listing of job openings and tips about the job application process.

U.S. Office of Personnel Management. www.usajobs.opm.gov. 1-202-606-252. Automated telephone system providing current worldwide federal job opportunities, salary and employee benefits information, and special recruitment messages. You can also record your request to have application packages, forms, and other employment-related literature mailed to you.

What Does the Future Hold?
Opportunities and Challenges

Rosy Outlook?

What does the future hold? On the one hand, the outlook seems good, but there are undoubtedly challenges ahead.

An article in *Firstline* rightly points out: "AAHA data shows turnover is almost 30 percent in veterinary practices, compared to a national average of 12 to 15 percent across all industries in the United States. And when they focused on technicians, the rate of turnover climbs to 35 percent... according to NAVTA, about 83 percent of their members say they'll probably or definitely stay in the profession. Yet 79 percent of NAVTA members and 85 percent of nonmembers agree that veterinary technicians are so underpaid that the feasibility of staying in the profession is declining" (Felsted 2008). But *Business Week* reports the following: "Americans now spend $41 billion a year on their pets, double the amount shelled out on pets a decade ago. . . . The yearly cost of buying, feeding, and caring for pets exceeds what Americans spend on the movies, playing video games, and listening to recorded music, combined" (Brady and Palmeri 2007). Further, occupational outlook handbooks show that "from 2008–2018, the demand for trained veterinary technicians is expected to increase faster than average for all other professions" (U.S. Bureau of Labor statistics). So where does that leave us?

Call to Action

Spending on pets and pet-related services continues to grow rapidly. At the same time, turnover is a problem in private practice.

Proactive steps can be taken to improve the future for veterinary medicine. The research for this book revealed large gaps in information about veterinary technicians.

For example, the growth projections are tough to analyze—although this profession has existed for 25 years, no one has yet collected data about the number of Credentialed Veterinary Technicians and technician assistants currently working in the field. This information is critical to evaluate supply and demand as well as turnover.

Additional information is needed to identify what tasks technicians and assistants actually perform. Change is in the air; it always is! Change is difficult for many people, and the doctor's delegating tasks to another person requires that there be clear communication and a solid base of skills and knowledge. As shifts occur in management and the focus changes from doctor-centered to client-centered practices, technicians with solid communication skills will excel and succeed. Another aspect to consider: there are roughly 30,000 veterinary hospitals in the United States and roughly 301 Certified Veterinary Practice Managers. This ratio seems out of proportion! When animal hospitals are well managed, with proper financial understanding, delegation of duties, and staffing, the veterinary community will achieve higher standards and pets will receive the best care.

In a well-managed hospital, doctors perform diagnosis, treatment, and surgery; technicians perform all the technical work allowed by law and directed by the veterinarian; and assistants help technicians with their tasks. Unfortunately, we still see doctors and technicians performing assistant work, such as holding an animal while blood is being drawn.

A related change involves two specific areas within veterinary medicine that are regulated loosely or not at all and that generate considerable controversy: animal massage and equine dentistry (see Chapter 3, "Traditional Veterinary Practice"). State regulations vary widely regarding who can legally perform these procedures; opinions vary widely about who is medically qualified to perform them. Unfortunately, as this debate rages, there is little information about where the interested technician can get reliable training in these fields.

Technician or nurse?

Those working within the veterinary profession may already know about the controversy regarding the word *nurse*. In Europe, Canada, and many other countries, the veterinary technician is called a nurse. In the United States, there has been resistance to using this term, both from nurses working in human medicine and from some people in veterinary medicine.

The word *nurse* is more comforting to a pet owner and instantly conjures up images of caring and nurturing. Of course, the veterinary technician's education also includes technology, such as laboratory procedures, surgical assistance, and inpatient and outpatient care. At the same time, technicians care for the pet in a comforting and nurturing way.

Another concern regarding nomenclature revolves around those team members who have less than an associate's degree in veterinary technology and work closely with Credentialed Veterinary Technicians. Common practice suggests these team members are titled *veterinary assistants*. There may be confusion among pet owners who are attempting to understand the duties of a veterinary assistant when they are familiar with the role of a physician's assistant (PA) in human medicine, who can diagnose and prescribe. We know that only a veterinarian can prescribe and diagnose in the veterinary community.

To help the general public understand titles within the veterinary community, changes in titles may occur so that a veterinarian diagnoses, prescribes medications, and performs surgery; the veterinary nurse (or even veterinary medical technician) receives direct orders from the veterinarian; and the veterinary aide (or clinical aide) assists the veterinary nurse in accomplishing those tasks. The human-animal bond may be the driving force for this change, unrelated to what the American Veterinary Medical Association or other professional groups may decide.

Veterinary technician specialties

Technicians who take their career to the specialty realm will be in high demand. Managers and veterinarians who understand the benefits of hiring and promoting veterinary technician specialists (VTSes) will elevate their services. VTSes will add another level of expertise, improving patient care, client communication, and client compliance. Managers have already embraced the concept in top-notch veterinary hospitals, recognizing the win/win atmosphere it creates with employees, doctors, and clients.

Use a career coach

Now more than ever, there are people and places to turn to for help moving your career forward. Your veterinary practice manager may encourage professional growth; if so, embrace this relationship. Also consider downloading a "Career Road Map" from www.myevt.com. Fill it out to identify your smart goals and take action! Some of you may be between opportunities for various reasons, and seeking advice from a career coach is a move in a positive direction. Dr. Beuscher of CoachVet offers this advice: "Your career as a veterinary technician and your advancement within an organization are directly proportional to your optimism and people skills. Winning relationships are built on a foundation of respect, trust, mutual benefit, and optimistic/uplifting attitudes."

Veterinary technician associations and professionalism

Now is the time for all veterinary technicians to join both their state and national veterinary technician associations. There is a renewed sense of professionalism, collaboration, and success among technicians and veterinary associations. Look for great things to come from the National Association of Veterinary Technicians in America, the American Animal Hospital Association, and the AVMA. Cooperation has never been better among the national organizations. Synergy has just begun and the possibilities are endless. With joined forces, resources, open minds, and collective passion, your associations can offer you benefits and support as never before. The challenge is for you to become active at your state level and support your national organization. Your career will benefit from belonging, no doubt about it!

Live Up to Your Potential

Throughout your career there will be opportunities to take the easy way out, to coast and just get by. There will also be those rare opportunities when you can test your skills, challenge yourself, and achieve great things. That's the difference between a career and a job. Coasting may keep you in the same grind, maintaining the status quo; however, challenging yourself will bring great rewards, personally and financially.

This is your challenge: "If I were courageous and set free of all boundaries, what would I do?" To feel the fear and do it anyway will bring your passions to life and fulfill your dreams.

A career in veterinary technology provides a wide array of choices. Within the environment of a veterinary hospital, you can take the reins and lead by example. You can work and embrace a career within a corporate industry, and you can also seek a career in detail-oriented research. Remember, too, all the options for self-employment and relief work.

Technicians must take it upon themselves to promote their own skills and assume responsibility for their financial goals. You may have heard that veterinarians are to be blamed for low pay and technician dissatisfaction, but technicians must take it upon themselves to create their own paths. When choosing a place of employment, identify its management style; seek out companies that have high retention, are progressive, and offer benefits. Investigate a company's reputation before accepting a job. Take charge of your life and make it exceptional in all aspects.

We wish you great success in all you do within your veterinary technician career.

Chapter Resources

Brady, Diane, and Christopher Palmeri. 2007. "The Pet Economy: Americans Spend an Astonishing $41 Billion a Year on Their Furry Friends." *Business Week*, August 6.

Felsted, Karen. 2008. "The Truth About the Technician Shortage: Will Low Salaries and High Turnover Threaten This Career?" *Firstline*, August 1. veterinaryteam .dvm360.com/firstline/article/articleDetail.jsp?id=542730.

Office of Occupational Statistics and Employment Projections. "Occupational Outlook Handbook, 2012–2013 Edition." U.S. Bureau of Labor Statistics. www.bls.gov/OCO. Accessed February 8, 2013.

About the Authors

Rebecca Rose, CVT

Rebecca Rose has spent her entire career within the field of veterinary medicine. She attributes her longevity in her profession to constantly reinventing herself, mentoring others, "thinking outside the box," and reaching new heights of excellence.

Offering leadership and guidance in different capacities to the Colorado Association of Certified Veterinary Technicians and the National Association of Veterinary Technicians in America has brought her great joy. Rose graduated from two Gunnison Valley leadership programs and one nine-month state-level leadership program. She enhances her leadership skills by participating in local political affairs, attending state veterinary and technician strategic planning, and acting as a facilitator to the Colorado State University first-year veterinary students as they participate in a three-day orientation.

The Colorado Veterinary Medical Association awarded her the Veterinary Technician of the Year Award in 2002, reflecting her professionalism and commitment to the veterinary community. In 2011 the Colorado VMA awarded her Industry Partner of the Year.

Working with various industry leaders throughout the years has forced Rose to step outside her comfort zone. Oftentimes she is asked for her input and expertise on veterinary technician delivery, collaboration, and networking.

Rebecca owns her own small business, Red Valley Rose Consulting. Classes provided by Rebecca include career choices, effective communication, professionalism, team delivery, and wealth management. She has presented at various state conventions, technician programs, and national events, most recently through the Veterinary Spport Personnel Network.

Her children and family support her in all of her endeavors. With their encouragement, she continually exceeds her own expectations, even surprising herself!

Please view her Web site at www.rebeccarosecvt.com for upcoming presentations, book information, and engagements.

Carin Smith, DVM

Dr. Carin Smith's career vision is to help veterinarians and their teams create successful lives and careers. She is a consultant, speaker, trainer, and author. She gained experience in both large- and small-animal practice before devoting her time to consulting.

Dr. Smith conducts workshops and gives presentations worldwide. Her workshops focus on "action learning," whereby skills and knowledge are immediately applied to real workplace situations. She is a certified mediator and a certified English language instructor.

Dr. Smith is a member of the Federal Executive Board, a group that conducts workplace mediation for the federal government. She is also a member of the American Society of Training and Development and the Society for Human Resource Management. She has served on the board of directors of the American Veterinary Medical Law Association and of VetPartners, a consultants' association.

Dr. Smith is a nationally recognized, award-winning author of hundreds of articles and many books, including *Career Choices for Veterinarians: Private Practice and Beyond*; *Client Satisfaction Pays: Quality Service for Practice Success*; *FlexVet: How to Be One, How to Hire One*; *The Comprehensive Practice Guide for Relief & Part-Time Veterinarians*; *The Housecall Veterinarian's Manual*; *The Relief Veterinary Technician's Manual* (with Rebecca Rose); and *Team Satisfaction Pays: Organizational Development for Practice Success*.

Please see Dr. Smith's Web site for complete details about Smith Veterinary Consulting, www.smithvet.com.

Index